Home Tonight

Further Reflections

on the Parable

of the

Prodigal Son

HENRI J. M. NOUWEN

Edited by Sue Mosteller, C.S.J.

Doubleday

New York   London   Toronto   Sydney   Auckland

DD

DOUBLEDAY

Copyright © 2009 by Henri Nouwen Legacy Trust

All Rights Reserved

Published in the United States by Doubleday, an imprint of
The Doubleday Publishing Group, a division of
Random House, Inc., New York.
www.doubleday.com

DOUBLEDAY and the DD colophon are registered trademarks of
Random House, Inc.

Book design by Songhee Oh

Library of Congress Cataloging-in-Publication Data

Nouwen, Henri J. M.
Home tonight : further reflections on the parable of the prodigal
son / by Henri J. M. Nouwen. —1st ed.
p. cm.
1. Prodigal son (Parable) 2. Spiritual life—Catholic Church.
I. Title.
BT378.P8N68 2008
248.4'82—dc22
2008032651

ISBN 978-0-385-52444-5

PRINTED IN THE UNITED STATES OF AMERICA

1 3 5 7 9 10 8 6 4 2

First Edition

Contents

Introduction

are you home tonight?

When Henri Nouwen first arrived at L'Arche Daybreak in 1986, he was asked to share a home with several people with intellectual dis abilities, one of whom was

We are not human beings on a spiritual journey. We are spiritual beings on a human journey.

Teilhard de Chardin.

John. Having lived many years in the community John is a rooted, grounded, middle-aged man in his group home of ten persons and his first question to any stranger is "So, where's your home?" Also wide-awake to the movements of each person around him, John daily asks assistants in his home and in the community a second, more immediate question: "Are you home tonight?" Henri, with his frenetic schedule, was not excused, especially from the second of these penetrating questions, and he very often had to falteringly explain to John why he would again be absent from the table that evening. Even though Henri initially came to Daybreak in search of a home, he needed more than the first year to discover the multifaceted meaning of "Where's your home?" and "Are you home tonight?" He needed this father figure, John, to firmly and consistently remind him that he was on a journey—home.

In the midst of his second year in the community Henri suffered a breakdown that took him away from L'Arche Daybreak for a period of seven months. He lived that time mostly in solitude and with the support of two friends from the Homes for Growth team in Winnipeg, Manitoba. I had the privilege of visiting him during his time there, and while sharing about his recovery he spoke movingly of his solitude and of his reflective "encounters" with the people in Rembrandt's painting of the prodigal son.

His experience was raw and deeply personal.

Fresh from his time in Winnipeg prior to his return to L'Arche Daybreak and more than three years before the publication of his classic book *The Return of the Prodigal Son,* Henri gave a three-day workshop about what had happened to him in his solitude with the Gospel story and the painting. Despite his struggle to put this experience into words, Henri took a risk and "found his voice" to describe what may be his best articulation of accepting himself as God's beloved son. He told this group of caregivers from L'Arche communities worldwide that his one desire in sharing as he did was to help each one of them to discover *their* personal connection between the parable and *their* own lives. Just as he had done in his solitude, he urged each one to make the prodigal son story his or her most intimate story.

Henri believed in his lis-
teners and trusted their
ability to move beyond his
experience to a personal,
unique, and precious en-
gagement with the parable
on their own. That same
confidence in the reader of

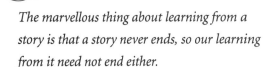

The marvellous thing about learning from a story is that a story never ends, so our learning from it need not end either.

From *The Active Life* by Parker J. Palmer, 1990, Harper and Row, San Francisco, p. 98.

this manuscript is evident even from beyond the grave, as he points the way for each of us to deeply and uniquely encounter Uncondi-tional Love through the scripture parable.

His conferences at the workshop were not taped professionally, but since his death, extracts from them have been reproduced and dis-tributed. Henri seems to have prepared his first conference with more attention than the second or third, and for this reason the exact tran-scription of the tapes has not been published. John Mogabgab and Robin Pippin from Upper Room Ministries in Nashville, Lindsey Yeskoo, a friend from Toronto, Trace Murphy at Doubleday in New York, and I accepted the challenge of editing the material in a way that gives Henri his authentic voice, captures his compelling testimony, and maps a way for each of us to an encounter of deep consequence.

Henri gave a talk each morning of the three-day workshop at the end of which he directed the participants to enter into quiet time and the practice of three ancient spiritual disciplines: listening, journal-ing, and communing. This personal spiritual workout was designed

I would like to beg you . . . as well as I can, to have patience with everything unresolved in your heart and to try to love the questions themselves as if they were locked rooms or books written in a foreign language. Don't search for the answers, which could not be given to you now, because you would not be able to live them. And the point is to live everything. Live the questions now. Perhaps then, someday, far into the future, you will gradually, without even noticing it, live your way into the answer.

From *Letters to a Young Poet* by Rainer Maria Rilke.

to enable each one to personally embrace and enter into the story and the painting for themselves. Later in the day in small groups, people listened to and shared their workout experiences with one another. Optional times of personal meditation and common worship were part of the schedule.

In keeping with this pattern, *Home Tonight* is designed to offer you the opportunity to step into the workshop experience and thus to hear the same voice that was more compelling than all of Henri's excuses, fears, and resistance.

It took a certain amount of courage for Henri to communicate his return *home* in spirit but somewhere he knew that his story carried the potential to bear fruit in the lives of others. What he didn't realize at the time, but what becomes more and more obvious as the talks unfold, is that Henri is gradually being transformed into the father figure he speaks about—the one who longs and hopes for our return as well.

So now, with Henri's "voice" to guide you and the living Spirit of Love to enflame you, it's your turn to listen personally to John's insightful questions, "Where's *your* home?" and "Are *you* home tonight?"

Sue Mosteller
Henri Nouwen Legacy Trust
August 2007

Prologue

walk with me into the story

From the outset I encourage you to allow the Scripture story of the return of the prodigal son to descend into you—to move from your mind into your heart—so that images in

Read with a vulnerable heart. Expect to be blessed in the reading. Read as one awake, one waiting for the beloved. Read with reverence.

From *A Tree Full of Angels* by Macrina Wiederkehr, 1991, Harper and Row, San Francisco, p. 53.

this story become etched in your spirit. I trust that something new will be born in you that is very different from what happened in me; something that is yours alone. Simply know that *how* you receive this parable is truly important. The parable and the painting are inviting you in, calling you to enter and participate as one of the characters. Choosing to be *part* of the story will allow you to become conscious of new connections with your own personal life journey, so I urge you to gradually allow the story to become your own most intimate story.

Furthermore, I urge you not to walk into the story alone, just in your own name. Rather, enter into the story in solidarity with all your brothers and sisters in the human family on earth. I honestly don't say this lightly, because I truly feel that you will enter into it well if you enter in the name of all those who share your humanity. Your desire to participate with those in the parable is not just good for you alone, but it is also good for many others because your personal life is a gift for the people immediately around you and beyond. We know now, especially from scientific research, that you and I are intimately related to everything and everyone in the universe. This is an invitation, then, to see yourself right here and right now "in the name" of many brothers and sisters, believing that as something moves in you, something may also transpire in those in whose name you live.

This may be new for you, but I encourage you to imagine yourself surrounded first by family and then by loved ones, relatives, friends, acquaintances, business associates, those in your neighborhood, church, culture, continent, and world. Perhaps some of the circles nearest you aren't easy for you. There are family struggles with spouses, parents, children, brothers, and sisters. There are many painful memories and feelings around breakages, losses, and communication struggles. Also, many other people near and far are in your consciousness; some doing well while others languish in poverty, sickness, abuse, violence, loneliness, famine, refugee camps, and despair. Bring them all around you, claim your humanity with them, never thinking or growing or speaking or acting just for yourself.

As you progressively become opened to others, allow all you choose in the most hidden places of your heart to be lived for all those who are alive *and* for those who have died. Gather them and keep them around you. You belong to every other person and to every particle of the universe. Like a stone thrown in the water, your life has ever-widening circles of relationship surrounding it. Enter the parable with all people in your heart. Call them around you, identify yourself with them, and let your thinking be deeply one with them as you journey with me into the story.

As we feel the pain of our own losses, our grieving hearts open our inner eye to a world in which losses are suffered far beyond our own little world of family, friends, and colleagues. It is the world of prisoners, refugees, AIDS patients, starving children, and the countless human beings living in constant fear. Then the pain of our crying hearts connects us with the moaning and groaning of a suffering humanity. Then our mourning becomes larger than ourselves.

From *With Burning Hearts*, by Henri J. M. Nouwen, 1999, Orbis Books, Maryknoll, NY, p. 28.

Throughout this book, where I often paraphrase when quoting from Scripture, I write of my personal experience *in* the parable of the prodigal son. If you understand my suffering and the joy out of which my words are born, you may then be able to take enough distance to say, "My life is different, but I find connections between those in the story and *my* story just as he did with his." I trust that as you engage the scriptural story you will let all my words go except what is relevant for you and your sacred relationship with God's creative Spirit.

Since I was very young my life has been dominated by two strong voices. The first said, "Make it in the world and be sure you can do it on your own." And the other voice said, "Whatever you do for the rest of your life, even if it's not very important, be sure you hold on to the love of Jesus." My father was a little more inclined to say the first and my mother the second. But the voices were strong. "Make your mark. Be able to show the world you can do it by yourself and that you are not afraid. Go as far as you want to go and be a man. Be a good older son and brother, and be sure you really do something relevant." And the other said, "Don't lose touch with Jesus, who chose a very humble and simple way. Jesus, by his life and death, will be your example for living."

I've struggled because one voice seemed to be asking me for upward mobility and the other for downward mobility and I was never sure how to do both at the same time.

I suppose that being the eldest son and part of a very ambitious family, I let the voice of upward mobility quickly win out. I initially *did* want to show the world I could do it, so I became a hyphenated priest. Do you know what a hyphenated priest is? Priest-psychologist. It wasn't enough to just be a priest. I wanted to be a psychologist too. Then if somebody didn't like priests, they might at least like psychologists! Thus I went on my upwardly mobile way. From Holland I went to the United States and soon went on to teach at Notre Dame. Then I went from Notre Dame to Yale, and from Yale to Harvard, and my father said, "Henri, you are doing very well!"

My mother, on the other hand, was asking, "Yes, but are you losing your connection with Jesus?"

Through it all, I've carried within me the pain of loneliness and a nagging need for affection. Although I loved teaching in the universities I was always yearning for intimacy in my life. I found this special love to a certain degree in my relationship with my mother. She loved me in a particular way, followed my every move, faithfully corresponded with me, expressing a love that was tangible, full, and close to being unconditional. When she died in 1978 during my time at

. . . I have entered deep waters,
and the flood sweeps over me.
I am exhausted from weeping;
I thirst as in a desert.
I no longer see the path while
Waiting for your return.

From *Psalms for Praying* by Nan C. Merrill, 1996, The Continuum International Publishing Group, New York, Psalm 69, p. 134.

Yale, I grieved her absence in a very profound place inside. Her love had always "held" me safe, but now it was gone. Her death was a double loss for me of both her person and also my whole sense of "home." Her absence plunged me into a downward spiral so that my final teaching years at Harvard in the early 1980s were some of the unhappiest of my life. It was there that I began an important life passage, from loneliness to L'Arche.

For the past year, I've been called into another, more challenging passage, from L'Arche to the second loneliness, and the parable of the prodigal son has companioned me along the way to a homecoming of large proportions. Now, quite simply, I desire to walk into this story with you as a potential entrance into a new passage of reclaiming something precious for you in your own life.

This story has the potential to be your most intimate story. It holds unique insights for you in this moment of your life. I only offer you my story to encourage you to claim your story, and to more seriously embrace your humanity in relationship with the One who created you. It is a call to engage your heart as well as your mind, and your life experience as well as your beliefs, to turn inward toward the unique "presence" that offers you safety, healing, forgiveness, and other important gifts.

To enable you in all of this you are invited to stop at certain intervals to engage in the practice of three ancient spiritual disciplines: listening, journaling, and communing. Each "spiritual workout" is a potential gateway for you to move beyond my story and more personally enter into the parable and the painting yourself. Similar to physical workouts that limber the body, spiritual disciplines support your fragile heart to bypass mere reading and to accept that you are being spoken to by the text in a most personal and specific way. Spiritual disciplines allow you to let the words descend from your mind into your heart, possess you, and live in you. They move you from learning about spiritual realities to encountering the living Spirit of Love. Regular spir-

. . . our familiarity may pose problems. These are stories from the Christian Scriptures that some of us have been hearing all our lives. They have been interpreted for us so often that our minds may be closed to new meanings.

From *The Active Life* by Parker J. Palmer, 1990, Harper and Row, San Francisco, p. 99.

itual workouts enliven you for the journey to integrity, the journey home.

The following story from Luke 15:11–32 provides the complete backdrop to my own story. Find a quiet, comfortable space, put aside preoccupations, and trust as you embark on the adventure of the spiritual disciplines. Read slowly. Drink it in. Let it soak into your bones. Allow it to flow freely from your mind into your heart.

Then [Jesus] said, There was a man who had two sons. The younger one said to his father, "Father, let me have the share of the estate that will come to me." So the father divided the property between them. A few days later, the younger son got together everything he had and left for a distant country where he squandered his money on a life of debauchery.

When he had spent it all, that country experienced a severe famine, and now he began to feel the pinch; so he hired himself out to one of the local inhabitants, who put him on his farm to feed the pigs. And he would willingly have filled himself with the husks the pigs were eating but no one would let him have them. Then he came to his senses and said, "How many of my father's hired men have all the food they want and more, and here am I dying of hunger! I will leave this place and go to my father and say: I have sinned against heaven and against you; I no longer deserve to be called your son; treat me as one of your hired men." So he left the place and went back to his father.

While he was still a long way off, his father saw him and was moved with pity. He ran to the boy, clasped him in his arms and kissed him. Then his son said, "Father, I have sinned against heaven and against you. I no longer deserve to be called your son." But the father said to his servants, "Quick! Bring out the best robe and put it on him; put a ring on his finger and sandals on his feet. Bring the calf we have been fattening, and kill it; we will celebrate by having a feast because this son of mine was dead and has come back to life; he was lost and is found." And they began to celebrate.

Now the elder son was out in the fields, and on his way back, as he drew near the house, he could hear music and dancing. Calling one of the servants he asked what it was all about. The servant told him, "Your brother has come, and your father has killed the calf we had been fattening because he has got him back safe and sound." He was angry then and refused to go in, and his father came out and began to urge him to come in; but he retorted to his father, "All these years I have slaved for you and never once disobeyed any orders of yours, yet you never offered me so much as a kid for me to celebrate with my friends. But for this son of yours, when he comes back after swallowing up your property—he and his loose women—you kill the calf we had been fattening."

The father said, "My son, you are with me always and all I have is yours. But it was only right we should celebrate and rejoice, because your brother here was dead and has come to life; he was lost and is found."

Consider what you have read as a sacred trust, as the gift of a fertile field full of yet-buried tiny seeds that need to be tended and watered so as to grow and bear fruit in you. Move forward in stillness.

Listening

You have read many words. Try not to be overwhelmed but rather focus on the one detail from the story that touches you more than the rest. Who is voicing that message? Why do you think it is meaningful for you? Stay attentive only to these stirrings in your heart.

Journaling

Mindful of what you feel, look at Rembrandt's masterful depiction of the parable on the inside flap of the cover of your book. Give your attention to how the light falls on the scene. Record in your journal all that you observe about the light. Stay with it, and write what you heard when you listened and what the light in the painting is saying to you. Take special note of the shadows and the darkness and write about them in contrast to

But it's not so simple, that sort of "quiet hour." It has to be learned. A lot of unimportant inner litter and bits and pieces have to be swept out first. Even a small head can be piled high inside with irrelevant distractions. True, there may be edifying emotions and thoughts, too, but the clutter is ever present. So let this be the aim of the meditation: to turn one's innermost being into a vast empty plain, with none of that treacherous undergrowth to impede the view so that something of "God" can enter you, and something of "Love," too.

From *An Interrupted Life, and Letters from Westerbork* by Etty Hillesum, 1996, Henry Holt and Company, New York, pp. 27–28.

the light. Find the words that express your thoughts and feelings about light, darkness, and shadows in your own life.

Communing

The exercise doesn't end at the tip of your pen, so put it down and allow yourself to move on. Imagine yourself before the One who loves you more than a daughter or a son, and speak your thoughts and feelings without fear. Lay them out as you would with a most trusted and cherished friend. Try to pinpoint your feelings and beliefs in terms of the light, darkness, and shadows you've encountered. It may be painful, but resolve to be completely honest, trusting that all you articulate will be heard without judgment and with loving compassion. Remain and be quietly present in the moment.

Heart speaks to heart.

part one

Leaving and Returning Home

1

from loneliness to l'arche

When I was at Harvard teaching about Jesus to hundreds of people from all over the world, I was miserable. It was then that I unconsciously touched the strong voice from my childhood that spoke to me about the simple way of Jesus. I began to wonder if my proclaiming the Gospel wasn't the best way of losing my very spirit and my connection with the Divine in my life. Harvard is a very ambitious institution, interested in the best and the

Suffering is a dreadful teacher but often the beginning of the best in us. Suffering and creativity are often interdependent. Pain produces a terrible tension released in our creative response. Suffering can be like a grain of sand in an oyster: it can create a magnificent pearl.

From *Straight from the Heart: Reflections from Twentieth-Century Mystics* by Dick Ryan, ed., 2001, Crossroad Publishing Company, New York, p. 158; quoted from *Teresa of Avila* by Tessa Bielecki, 1994, Crossroad Publishing Company.

brightest, in power, upward mobility, political influence, and economic success. Talking about Jesus there wasn't easy and I felt pressure to adopt the model of the university, to become more competitive and to "make it" as a professor in that environment. Separated by death from the loving relationship with my mother, I also felt very lonely, detached in prayer, unable to respond to those who wanted to become my friends, and without a community around me. I knew that I *had* to do something, but I felt desperate because I didn't know what to do. I began to ask Jesus in times of prayer for directions out of my pain.

One morning in my little apartment a knock came at the door. The little woman standing on the step smiled at me. "Hello," I said. "What are you doing here so early in the morning?"

"Well," she answered, "my name is Jan Risse."

"What can I do for you?"

"Well, I've come to bring you greetings from Jean Vanier."

Now the name Jean Vanier was just a name for me. I admired his communities, called L'Arche, that welcomed people with disabilities, and I had even mentioned Jean Vanier in one of my books. But I had never met him. So again I said to Jan Risse, "What can I do for you?"

She continued to smile and replied, "Well, I come to bring greetings from Jean Vanier."

"Thank you so much. I really appreciate that. So, what is it that you really come for?" I asked.

"Well, I come to bring greetings from Jean Vanier."

Conscious of my busy day ahead and hoping to bypass the small talk, I said, "Did you want me to give a lecture somewhere, or give a seminar, or a talk? What can I do for you?" She looked at me and suggested that I invite her to come in! I stood aside and said, "Sure, you can come in, but I have a class and then I have a meeting and I'm completely tied up until suppertime."

In my living room she turned and said, "OK, that's fine. You go off and I'll be fine right here until your return." Thus, she came in and I left for the better part of the day. Upon my return in the early evening I gazed at my room. The table was covered with a white linen cloth and beautifully set with candles, a bottle of wine, fine china, and flowers in the center. Astonished I exclaimed, "What's this?"

"Oh, I thought you and I could have dinner together," she casually replied.

"But where did you find all these beautiful things?" I asked.

"From your own cupboard!" she said, pointing to the buffet. "You must not look around your own house very often!" She had created this wonderful dinner for the two of us with candles and wine—from my own house!

I found her a room on campus and she stayed for three days. We had a few visits and she came to my classes and then she left. Her last words to me were "Remember, Jean Vanier sent his greetings."

I sat in my chair and said to myself, "Something is happening. This visit wasn't for nothing." But then nothing happened for many, many months until the phone rang one day and Jean Vanier was on the other end of the line. "Henri," he said, "I'm on a retreat here in Chicago and I was thinking of you. Is there any chance you could come and join us here?"

Whatever happens to me in life,
I must believe that somewhere,
In the mess or madness of it all,
There is a sacred potential—
A possibility for wondrous redemption
In the embracing of all that is.

From *Straight from the Heart: Reflections from Twentieth-Century Mystics* by Dick Ryan, ed., 2001, Crossroad Publishing Company, New York, p. 85; quoted from *A Mystical Heart* by Edwina Gateley, Crossroad Publishing House.

I hastened to reply, "Jean, I have already given a number of retreats this year."

Jean answered, "I'm not asking you to give the retreat. I'm here on a retreat with a number of people from L'Arche worldwide, and I just thought you might like to be here to pray with us. We're all in silence, so you don't have to worry about talking to lots of people. You and I could visit and it might be a rest for you."

Almost immediately the same sense that something important was happening prompted me to drop everything and go to Chicago for several days. Nobody was talking, but more than fifty people were together there for conferences, meals, sharing, and worship. Apart from a daily visit with Jean in which I shared my angst in Harvard, I enjoyed a silent retreat with people from L'Arche around the world. When it was time to leave I felt rested as well as challenged by something Jean Vanier had said to me in passing at one point: "Perhaps our people [i.e., people with disabilities who live in L'Arche] could offer you a home."

That one sentence touched a chord in me and seemed like a prophetic call, so I visited Jean in his L'Arche home just north of Paris the next time I went to Europe. I felt relaxed with the people with disabilities and in general I experienced peace, rest, and safety in the community. I knew Harvard wasn't the place for me, so I resigned at the end of the year and took a writing sabbatical in Jean's community at Trosly. While I was there, the L'Arche Daybreak community in Toronto, Canada, called me to come

Bit by intelligible bit, a vocation lets us express our healthiest instincts, our noblest desires. . . . In small things and in large, we can attend to the haunting inner summons of our soul.

From *Straight from the Heart: Reflections from Twentieth-Century Mystics* by Dick Ryan, ed., 2001, Crossroad Publishing Company, New York, p. 85; quoted from *Holy Work*, by Marsha Sinetar, 1989, Crossroad Publishing House.

there for three years as their pastor and I said "yes" to their invitation.

The following year I found a wonderful home at Daybreak, and there completed the first part of my journey from loneliness to L'Arche. But it was a surprise to discover that there was still a way to go. A long way.

In my L'Arche formation the word most used was the word "home." L'Arche is a home. Jean had said to me, "Maybe our people can offer you a 'home.' " Daybreak was saying, "Our community wants you to be pastor, and we think we can offer you a 'home.' " Because my life had always been lived alone and because of inner loneliness, that word, "home," touched me in my heart. In the competitive world of the university, "home" was not a significant word. "Institution," "success," "financial gain," and "power" obliterate the concepts of "community," "intimacy," and "togetherness."

Because I was longing for belonging and a sense of home, I came to L'Arche filled with new hope of finding fulfillment. It was a shock for me during the first three years at L'Arche to gradually realize that "home" might mean something other than what my heart craved and my flesh desired. I was under the illusion that home was the pure experience of warmth, intimacy, and affection, and at the beginning there was a lot of that. But the longer I lived at Daybreak the more I realized that I might have to give up home in order to find it. While living with handicapped people and their assistants at Daybreak I sensed that the Lord was inviting me to something that I was certainly not ready to live.

As I lived longer in the Daybreak community old demons around my need for affection revisited me, and I began to find it difficult to love freely without being selfish and demanding. I sensed myself going into a dark tunnel leading to a second loneliness unlike anything I had ever lived before. I don't have many words to describe what happened to me, but the story of the prodigal son will help me unwrap for you the gift and spiritual significance of this, my journey.

Reading the story and studying the painting of the prodigal son brought me to recognize that there is a younger child in me that needs conversion, and there

Healing begins when, in the face of our own darkness, we recognize our helplessness and surrender our need for control . . . we face what is, and we ask for mercy.

From *Straight from the Heart: Reflections from Twentieth-Century Mystics* by Dick Ryan, ed., 2001, Crossroad Publishing Company, New York, p. 78; quoted from *Prayer and the Quest for Healing: Our Personal Transformation and Cosmic Responsibility* by Barbara Fiand, 1999, Crossroad Publishing Company.

is an elder sibling in me that needs conversion as well. Most importantly, however, I realized there is a father, a parent, that needs to be first revealed in me and then claimed by me, in order for *me* to receive the younger and the elder children that long, like me, to come home. Because of this experience with the parable, I feel more confident that a time will come when we will all share the celebration—not only of the return of many younger prodigals, but also the return of the elder daughters and sons to the home of their true identities as siblings and parents around the table with the Father-Mother-God. The word "home," more than anything else, called me to move forward on my journey to share my life with others in L'Arche.

So on my journey from loneliness to L'Arche I was finally paying attention to my life and to the internal and external "happenings and events" that pointed me to life changes. "Being attentive to the signs" is a wisdom practice handed down through the generations from our very wise and holy ancestors.

Listening

These exercises happen within the sacred context of your life. You are invited to listen with your heart as well as with your mind.

Find a quiet space and become comfortable. Look at Rembrandt's painting and gently step into the painted scene as an invisible guest. Situate yourself in the place in the room where you feel most comfortable as an onlooker. Close your eyes and become aware of the sounds in the room. What noises are you hearing? What voices do you hear? Take time to listen to the unfolding scene—from within.

Journaling

Still in the portrait, open your journal and write what you see and hear. Take your time. Then focus and take note of the feelings your presence there evoked in you. Write how each person and their words affected you. Write what you feel and how your heart responds.

We know that there is an enormous power inherent in each of us, at every moment in time, to experience the unbounded love and deep joy which is potentially our inheritance.

From *Always We Begin Again: The Benedictine Way of Living* by John McQuiston II, 1996, Morehouse Publishing, Harrisburg, PA, p. 80.

Communing

Go to the privileged place in your heart where no one but you and your God have access. Articulate to the One who fashioned you and who is with you always, even to the end of time, your experience as participant in the parable.

Stop and listen for the still, small voice of Love. Speak again, then wait and listen. Remain. Abide. Rest.

Heart speaks to heart.

A Wisdom Practice for Those on a Spiritual Journey

Practice #1   BE ATTENTIVE TO THE "SIGNS"

Feeding the pigs and close to despair, the runaway prodigal knew that his life *had* to change. A certain hope was born when he considered going home, but that was soon replaced by shame, fear, and the utter impossibility of such a simple move. But his options were limited, so glimmerings of excitement around thoughts of "home" persisted. Because he listened, he was one day able to turn with uneasy confidence and begin his journey home.

In those final years at Harvard I also "knew" that teaching in the university was deadening. I prayed, sought advice, and tried to be attentive to inner movements indicating what was to be next for me. Connecting first with Jan Risse and then with Jean Vanier moved me in my heart, and I knew that our meetings were not accidental. I listened. Although the initial idea of moving to L'Arche excited me, it was still with reluctance, fear, and uneasy confidence that I left the university and haltingly stepped into the impossible.

To live authentically each

Don't surrender your loneliness so quickly.
Let it cut more deep.
Let it ferment and season you,
As few human or even divine ingredients can.
Something missing in my heart tonight
Has made my eyes soft,
My voice, so tender,
My need for God,
Absolutely clear.

Shams al-Din Hafiz.

of us must be aware of our "within." We need to become conscious of feeling content, safe, and in the right place, and of feeling lonely, disillusioned, or mildly depressed. In front of turmoil, what do we do? Wise teachers tell us to be *very* attentive at these moments, to be open to "signs," feelings, comments, a line in a book, unexpected meetings or events that may move us to consider new directions, to refind balance, and to remain fully alive. Spiritual signs usually have four characteristics: They are simple not complicated, persistent, seemingly impossible, and always about others as well as ourselves. Be attentive when you experience these on your journey. Try to recognize an opportunity as well as a difficulty. Try not to respond too quickly. Pray for wisdom. Seek advice and refuse to act until you have external affirmation for your direction. Take time to believe in your free choice before you move forward in a new direction.

2

the younger son

I am a Dutchman. Rembrandt is a Dutchman and van Gogh is a Dutchman. These Dutch painters have entered into my heart in a very deep way, so I have them in mind as I speak to you. They have become my consolation and when I find I have nothing else to say, when I have only tears for what is happening in my life, I look at Rembrandt or at van Gogh. Their lives and their art heal and console me more than anything else.

All artists must learn the art of surviving loss: loss of hope, loss of face, loss of money, loss of self-belief . . . Artistic losses can be turned into artistic gains and strengths—but not in isolation of the beleaguered artist's brain. . . . We must acknowledge it and share it.

From *The Artist's Way: A Spiritual Path to Higher Creativity* by Julia Cameron, 1992, Jeremy P. Tarcher/Putnam, New York, p. 129.

Rembrandt painted the picture of the prodigal son between 1665 and 1667, at the end of his life. As a young painter, he was popular in Amsterdam and successful with commissions to do portraits of all the important people of his day. He was known as arrogant and argumentative, but he participated in the circles of the very rich in society. Gradually, however, his life began to deteriorate:

> First he lost a son,
> then he lost his first daughter,
> then he lost his second daughter,
> then he lost his wife,
> then the woman he lived with ended up in a mental
>   hospital,
> then he married a second woman who died,
> then he lost all his money and fame, and
> just before he himself died, his son Titus died.

It was a man who experienced immense loneliness in his life that painted this picture. As he lived his overwhelming losses and died many personal deaths, Rembrandt could have become a most bitter, angry, resentful person. Instead he became the one who was finally able to paint one of the most intimate paintings of all time—*The Return of the Prodigal Son.* This is not the painting he was able to paint when he was young and successful. No, he was only able to paint the mercy of a blind father when he had lost everything: all of his children but one, two of his wives, all his money, and his good name and popularity. Only after that was he able to paint this picture, and he painted it from a place in himself that knew what God's mercy was. Somehow his loss and suffering emptied him out to receive fully and deeply the mercy of God. When Vincent van Gogh saw this painting he said, "You can only paint this painting when you have died many deaths." Rembrandt could do it only because he had died so many deaths that he finally knew what the return to God's mercy really meant.

We can look back over Rembrandt's life and witness his personal and artistic transformation. If it touches us, it is important for us to consider our own story, and to take our own lives very seriously.

I became aware of how important the Rembrandt painting was for me when, just prior to my becoming pastor at L'Arche Daybreak in 1986, a friend called me and said, "I'm going to Russia. Would you like to come with me?" My immediate response was, "Oh, how amazing! I'm going to see Rembrandt at the Winter Palace of Peter the Great!" I didn't say anything about Moscow or the Kremlin. I'm ashamed to say that I wasn't even thinking of Russian people, or Russian culture, or even Russian icons. I was thinking about Rembrandt because I knew this painting was in the Hermitage Museum in Leningrad and I knew I wanted to see the real thing.

After we arrived in Russia and with some effort, I finally connected with the restorer in the Hermitage Museum. I told him, "I want to see that painting. That's all. I don't want to pass by it in a line of people but I want to sit in front of it for as long as I want to sit there! I don't want anything else!" He kindly took me directly to the painting, eight feet high and covering one wall of the museum, and he put me right in front of it. I sat in one of the three velvet chairs before the

*All life is a beginning. I need an open, sponta-
neous, joyful attitude that knows it does not
know. I need an emptiness in me . . . I need to
find the part in my soul still empty, still able to
be surprised, still open to wonder.*

From *The Finding Stone* by Christine Lore Weber,
1995, Lura Media, San Diego.

painting and I stared to my heart's content. I studied the painting carefully and then began making notes while whole crowds of people came, stopped for a moment, and passed by.

By two o'clock in the afternoon when the sun on the painting caused a glare, I took my chair and shifted it to another position. Before I could sit down the guard approached me and in a commanding way said in Russian something like, "This chair goes *there!*" He picked it up and put it in its original spot. I tried to tell him, distinctly moving my lips and pointing to the window, "But I can't see anything. Look, can't you see the glare? I *have* to sit here!" He shook his head, stating again, "No, the chair goes *there!*" Finally, in desperation, I said to myself, "Forget about it," and I sat down on the floor. To the guard this move turned out to be a much greater sin than moving the chair in the first place. So he came racing back, looked down at me on the floor, and said, "You can't sit on the floor!" He pointed and said, "Sit on the radiator!" I got up and settled myself uncomfortably on the radiator.

Soon the next large group of people appeared, and when the tour guide saw me on my perch she looked aghast and hastened to indicate to me, "You're not allowed to sit on the radiator!" But then the guard jumped back in and told her in no uncertain terms, "I gave him permission to sit on the radiator!" Fortunately, while the two of them were fighting it out, Alexi, the restorer for the whole museum, came by to see how I was doing. He recognized my confusion and entered into conversation to quiet the guard and the guide. Then, without speaking to me, he left, followed by the guide and the tour group. After about ten minutes Alexi returned carrying a velvet chair, which he set down before me, saying, "This is your own chair! You can move it wherever you like."

I sat before the painting for three days, two or three hours a day, pondering, studying, reflecting, and making notes. The more I looked, the more I became part of the story, and I began to make connections between the Gospel parable and my own personal life. I was deeply aware of the return; the return to the womb of the Divine Creator.

The life force I saw was more than a father. The Divine I saw was also a Mother. I knew in my heart how the reminder by Jesus to become like a child, so as to enter into the kingdom, was portrayed as a return to the womb of God. I also felt that my whole future would depend on my willingness to reenter the womb of my Creator-God and to find my home there. This was a welcome confirmation of my decision to allow the people of L'Arche Daybreak to help me make my return home in body and spirit.

All human nature vigorously resists grace because grace changes us and the change is painful.

From *The Habit of Being* by Flannery O'Connor, 1979, Vintage Books, New York. p. 307.

After my return from Russia I began my life as pastor at L'Arche Daybreak—my choice of home. I had made a conscious decision that my spiritual focus for the first year would be finding my center and home in the One who had created me and who loves me with unfathomable love. I began to reflect on my life with the painting and the parable as my context.

Although I myself am the oldest child in my family, I still feel there is a lot of that young man in the painting in me. There's a part of me that always wants to break away from a good thing, to break away from home. Although I've always had a good home and an OK father and mother, there remains in me a young adolescent urging me to cut loose. "I want to break out, discover forbidden things for myself and I don't want to hear forbidding voices. I want to get what belongs to me and run with it."

This adolescent attitude of wanting to find my own answers, solve my own problems, and discover my own truth is natural, so people who try to give me

So here is the paradox: as humans we are caught between competing drives, the drive to belong, to fit in and be a part of something bigger than ourselves, and the drive to let our deepest selves rise up, to walk alone, to refuse the accepted and the comfortable, and this can mean, at least for a time, the acceptance of anguish. It is in the group that we discover what we have in common. It is as individuals that we discover a personal relationship with God. We must find a way to balance our two opposing impulses.

From *Becoming Human* by Jean Vanier, 1998, House of Anansi Press, Toronto, pp. 18–19.

answers before I'm even looking for them irritate me. The parental voices speak, "This is how to behave. This is how to relate. This is how to worship. This is how to do this and not do that. This is the school for you." To hell with all that!

> I want to live my own life without parental voices.
> I don't want to have answers before I even raise the questions.
> I don't want to have religion before I even have a need for it.
> I don't want to be given all the right ways before I've learned on my own about wrongdoing.
> I don't want answers coming to me from a place that is pre-given.

How can something really become mine when I haven't accepted it from within? How can I appreciate home when I wasn't looking for home because I have no other options than the home I already have? I hear myself complaining, "Don't you know that my life is full of questions? Can't you see that I want to say 'yes' to my own truth from within? I don't want what is premade. I want to build my own home and I don't want a prefab home that someone who doesn't even know me has made." My psychological training made me know very well what that was all about.

This phase is about self-discovery and self-expression. Because adolescence holds all the dangers of getting lost, the parents become justifiably afraid. *They* know what is right. They know how I should

I do not act as I mean to, but I do things that I hate . . . for though the will to do what is good is in me, the power to do it is not.

From the Jerusalem Bible, Romans 7:15–18.

eat. They know how I should talk. They know how I should walk. They know what I should and shouldn't do. And it's true. They do know a lot because they have lived longer than I have. So their concern is natural and good. At the same time everything in me is saying, "Forget it! I no longer want all that. It's my life, not yours. Let me go free." And I know that my feelings are natural and good.

I come from a background that is very traditional Catholic. Everything in our home was crystal clear. Nothing was ambiguous. We were well taught all the essentials: how we socialized, how we met new people, how we prayed, how we worshipped, and how we studied! I remember very vividly at the time how jealous I was of those who had no religion. They could do anything they wanted and they didn't even feel guilty about it! All I could do was say, "Hell, I've already been told I'm not to do this and I should do that, I'm not allowed to go there and I'm supposed to go here, this is the way to behave and that is not!" Meanwhile I saw people who couldn't care less. They did everything and anything with their minds, with their bodies, with other people, and they seemed perfectly free. So I was jealous. I wanted to be a pagan so I could do all the things I wanted to do and not feel guilty.

But that wasn't for me. I can thank my parents for my education, for encouraging me to make good friends, for a healthy body, and for a good and true family. But every time I did something wrong, I ended up feeling guilty! I didn't want to feel guilty, but damn it, my parents raised me with so much clarity around right and wrong that whatever I did I was always in trouble and full of bad feelings besides. I vividly remember the inner dialogue:

"OK, I want to become a Christian, but first I want to do all the things I'm not supposed to do so that I can be converted. OK, I'm willing to discover that maybe some things are questionable, but let me find that out by myself. I don't want anyone to tell me what is good and what is no good. What I need is to go out, to travel, and to move. So just give me my stuff, let me go, and trust that I can discover what I need to know on my own. Why, since I was a little baby, did I already have to be a little priest?"

I really wish my parents had recognized how natural it is to want to cut loose and to travel and to do something other than what they consider to be decent or appropriate.

Much of my adolescent "breaking out" bothered my conscience with feelings of guilt and fear as to how to get back on track as soon as possible. I began my return as well as I could and in

I live in confusion and despair
because of my anguish;
My body responds with illness
because of my stubbornness,
Ignorance casts me into darkness, and
I grope in every direction,
searching in vain.

From *Psalms for Praying* by Nan C. Merrill, 1996, The Continuum International Publishing Group, New York, Psalm 38, p. 72.

faith but I continued to slip backwards: "I'm a beloved child, returning home where I belong, but my Maker will probably be furious and never want to see me again." I imagined being shouted at for having been given so much, for not becoming a lawyer or getting a real job. I projected that I'll be told to get out and never come back! Finally, I began to prepare my speech. "I'm just your miserable little child, and maybe you can give me a little morsel of food because I'm so miserable." I revert to old patterns of projecting God's reaction from the place of my failure. That is my repeated experience of trying to return home.

Perhaps you who read this book can identify with my wavering returns. You believe you have an identity and you know who you are, but you don't know, either, because you feel so insecure. Perhaps you, too, run for affirmation, affection, or success. Perhaps you don't know clearly what exactly you seek, but you experience an angst that holds you back from feeling truly free. You, too, may be afraid to open yourself to the unconditional love of the One who "formed you in your mother's womb." You might ask yourself why you are always busy and seldom still, always running and complaining at the same time of having no time to simply be.

There are psychoanalytic theories about why Christians become violent against others. It is as if we are angry that we haven't really chosen or experienced or integrated our faith for ourselves. We received it often as a burden that is difficult to reject because of the learned consequences.

The Scripture story of the prodigal son recounts his taking his inheritance and leaving home to spend it all on women, games, and gambling. He's going to test drive the pleasures of life in a foreign land and away from familiar teaching voices. In the secret of his heart he's probably saying to himself, "Whatever am I doing? This isn't very smart. In fact, it's ridiculous." As he loses it all, he knows how stupid he is. On the other hand, isn't this exactly what he has to do in order to finally claim what for himself is truly real? And isn't he learning about his false and his true self?

Rabbi Levi saw a man running in the street, and asked him, "Why do you run?" He replied, "I am running after my good fortune!" Rabbi Levi tells him, "Silly man, your good fortune has been trying to chase you, but you are running too fast."

From *Sabbath: Restoring the Sacred Rhythm of Rest* by Wayne Muller, 1999, Bantam Books, New York, p. 48.

Perhaps each of us might take a moment to identify with the prodigal. Perhaps we are able to remember times when we consciously knew the truth of what our parents, teachers, and friends were saying, but we said it was dumb and stupid and we rationalized, "Well, you can all tell me that, but right now I need to find out for myself."

While the young man in the story seemingly left his home and lost everything, one possession remained. He was still a *member* of his family. He *belonged* to those people and to that homestead. As he moved through the pain of his disillusionment with life and himself to the awareness that there was something that could never be lost, he began his actual return. "I'm still the child of my father and of my mother. I still *belong* to my family. I still have a home where people who know me are alive." Hidden below all these thoughts is an enormous load of confusion, guilt, and shame because he knows he has acted stupidly and is now at the bottom. He has few options. He can only choose to live in despair or to reach out to reclaim his truth. From deep within he opts to turn and to return. "Let me go back to my father's house."

He's not immediately able to claim the whole truth however. While he is saying "I'll go home," he is not saying "My parents will be happy to see me back and will receive me with open arms." Not even close! The most he is able to say is "I'm going home to the place where I belong and my family has servants who have more food than I'm getting here. I will just say, 'Father, I've sinned against you, and so why don't you treat me at least like you treat the servants.'" So on one hand he claims his truth about having a true home and turns back, but on the other hand, confused and blinded with guilt, he hasn't much freedom at all. At least he claims it, though, and it is enough for him to turn and return.

Jesus made the connection about his belonging in his baptism when he heard the Father's incredible affirmation of his person. "You are my favorite

I hear my Beloved.
See how he comes leaping on the mountains,
Bounding over the hills,
My Beloved is like a gazelle, like a young stag.

See where he stands behind our wall.
He looks in at the window,
He peers through the lattice.

My Beloved lifts up his voice, he says to me,
Come then, my love, my lovely one, come.
For see, winter is past, the rains are over and
  gone.

From the Jerusalem Bible, Song of Songs, 2:8–11.

son. In you I am well pleased." This knowledge of his primal truth made it possible for him to live his life and to accept his death in a world of both acceptance and rejection, without ever losing his deep affiliation with the One who sent him into the world. He knew the truth. He claimed himself in truth so that whether people wanted to be with him, listen to him, make him king, reject him, beat him, spit on him, or nail him to the Cross, he never lost the truth that he was God's beloved child.

This same connection and lack thereof is demonstrated as well in the stories of Peter and Judas. Both were given a place in the company of Jesus and it was, for them, an identity. They were chosen and they knew it. Yet both left their truth through denial and betrayal. At the moment of realization, Peter reclaimed his identity as friend of Jesus and wept in sorrow. Judas, however, unable to claim equality with people who hadn't been overtly sinful, became suicidal, renounced his inheritance, and hanged himself.

You and I know spiritually about belonging, leaving, and returning. We, like the young prodigal, can learn to act ahead of our feelings, trust that love is there, and make our shaky return. And we will do it more readily if we come to know the God figure in the story. Before now I was never able to see how the love of the father embraced not just the return of his younger child but also his running away from home. That is an enlightening consideration prompting me now to question, "Do you mean you were actually *there* in my leaving?" and "Does this mean that I can come home and you'll still be there for me?"

Perhaps the whole movement of leaving and returning is only one movement rather than two, especially as it is experienced in the loving heart of the father. This is not a parent who says, "Don't go." That kind of statement is not in keeping with the spirit of this story. The spirit of the story is different. It reads, "Yes, son. Go. And you will be hurt and it will be hard, and it will be painful. And you might even lose your life, but I will not hold you back from taking that risk. When and if you come back, I am always here for you. But I'm also here for you now in your leaving. Yes, we belong together and I am never separated from you." This aspect of Love Divine is, for me, a critical life-connection.

I feel that in our hearts it's good to be convinced somewhere of the merciful One's love and to risk leaving occasionally. Isn't it true that there are times for us, as in the life of the younger son, when we simply need to go off for a while? I believe the Giver of Life loves each of us as a daughter or a son who is leaving and returning constantly. The more we become sensitive to our own journey the more we realize that we are leaving and coming back every day, every hour. Our minds wander away but eventually return; our hearts leave in search of affection and re-

Teach me, that I may know my weaknesses,
the shortcomings that bind me,
The unloving ways that separate me,
that keep me from recognizing
your life in me.
For, I keep company with fear, and
dwell in the house of ignorance.
Yet, I was brought forth in love,
and love is my birthright.

From *Psalms for Praying* by Nan C. Merrill, 1996, The Continuum International Publishing Group, New York, Psalm 52, p. 102.

turn sometimes broken; our bodies get carried away in their desires then sooner or later return. It's never one dramatic life moment but a constant series of departures and returns.

Having lived my own encounter with the story and the painting, I feel empowered to invite you to claim your leaving and returning home with compassion. We are beloved children of our Maker. We are held safe by everlasting and unending love. It's normal, then, for us in growing up spiritually to live according to our nature. "Yes, I'm loved, even when I take a risk to satisfy my desire to claim my life. I'm loved, even if I make mistakes. I may have acted badly but I didn't have any other way to do it at that moment. People have hurt me and I've suffered unjustly, but I am loved before anything happened to me." This is important so as not to judge ourselves more harshly than the One who loves us.

When we do not claim the presence of love in our departures, we experience a guilt-ridden return to a dark God, reprimanding us, saying, "I always knew you would fail. I could have told you that you would need me again." This is not the image of the Great Creator in the prodigal's story. God is not laughing because we couldn't do it on our own. The Spirit is not demanding that we finally confess in guilt and shame as a condi-

A spiritual discipline . . . is the concentrated effort to create some inner and outer space in our lives . . . A spiritual discipline sets us free to pray, or to say it better, allows the Spirit of God to pray in us.

From *Making All Things New* by Henri Nouwen, 1981, HarperSanFrancisco, San Francisco, p. 68.

tion of our return. The God in the parable is a personal, intimate, and loving Presence who lets each of us go and welcomes each one home, all in amazing generosity and forgiveness. This reflection isn't an intellectual exercise about right and wrong. More, it is an opening of ourselves to gradually let go of fear, to trust anew, and to make space for the love of the One who both blesses our leaving and waits to celebrate our return.

Listening

In a quiet moment open yourself to listen to the story in a whole new way. This time approach the written parable from the perspective of posture. Ready yourself to be surprised and listen for what the given positions suggest to you.

Reflect on each main character in the painting and ask yourself what you learn about these individuals from the way the artist portrayed them in that one moment in time. Ponder what Jesus may be trying to convey in the story. Read your own meaning into the characters.

Journaling

Again let pen meet paper and take time to describe your portrayal of the younger son's position in the painting and in the story. What does his posture tell you about the condition of his heart? Write any feelings of inner or outer identification with him. Continue to write, mindful of some of your own leavings and returnings, even if they are painful. Try to capture your experience and your feelings in words without looking for perfection. Stay with the real question and write. As a daughter or son, what is stirred in you because of this young man?

Communing

Voice your heart's response to the One who, no matter how great the ache, allowed you the space to leave without revoking the blessing. And if you are still away, voice the feelings evoked in your heart right now.

If you remember the ever-outstretched arm extended to you in unrestrained welcome, and if you ever feel the hand of Unconditional Love set itself securely on your back, give thanks for being safely *home* once again.

Heart speaks to heart.

I learned to get out of the way and let the creative force work through me. I learned to just show up at the page and write down what I heard. Writing became more like eavesdropping and less like inventing a nuclear bomb. . . . I didn't have to be in the mood. I didn't have to take my emotional temperature to see if inspiration was pending. I simply wrote. No negotiations. Good? Bad? None of my business. I wasn't doing it. By resigning as the self-conscious author, I wrote freely.

From *The Artist's Way: A Spiritual Path to Higher Creativity* by Julia Cameron, 1992, Jeremy P. Tarcher/Putnam, New York, pp. xiv–xv.

We keep silence. Help us to save ourselves by forgetting ourselves. In every experience and thought, bring us to the certain knowledge that we are children of the infinite.

From *Always We Begin Again: The Benedictine Way of Living* by John McQuiston II, 1996, Morehouse Publishing, Harrisburg, PA, p. 74.

A Wisdom Practice for Those on a Spiritual Journey

Practice #2 CELEBRATION

"A festival is a sign of heaven. It symbolises our deepest aspiration—an experience of total communion." (Vanier, Jean. *Community and Growth*, London: Darton, Longman, and Todd, 2nd revised edition, 1989.) The old father in the parable spontaneously knew the appropriate response to a long-desired homecoming. He ordered the servants to "kill the fatted calf and prepare a feast." We aren't told whether or not the contrite runaway was ready to be celebrated as "a beloved with whom there is total communion." But we often can identify with a certain shameful reluctance in ourselves to be celebrated with similar unconditional affection.

In the university setting I lost the real meaning of "festival," but the simple gestures of love and affirmation at Daybreak remind me that celebration is much more than a party or a spectacle. I'm touched when we pause at the end of a delicious, noisy birthday meal and each one announces to the celebrant unique gratitude for his or her life. I'm moved when following a death we gather to tell stories, laugh, cry, and remember together. I'm touched each spring when Ellen's parents arrive with several others from the Khahila to share the Seder supper and point us to God's presence through the history of the "chosen people." And there is real joy when Friday night worship ends and people spontaneously begin to dance during the final hymn! Celebrating is rejoicing in friendship, lifting a glass because of it, affirming each other, and knowing gratitude in our hearts.

As a spiritual discipline of love, celebration is, beyond partying and entertaining, a well-prepared meeting of wonderment and friendship. Utilize your creativity to fashion simple "fiestas" to overtly affirm, bless, and lift up a loved one. And when you are the one being celebrated, really try to be simple and receive true nourishment for your unsteady heart.

from l'arche to a second loneliness

Sing and dance together and be joyous,
but let each one of you be alone.
Even as the strings of a lute are alone
though they quiver with the same music.
Stand together yet not too near together
for the pillars of the temple stand apart,
and the oak tree and the cypress
grow not in each other's shadow.

From *The Prophet* by Kahlil Gibran, 1951, Alfred A. Knopf, New York, pp. 15–16.

My honeymoon at L'Arche lasted a little more than a year. Then the old demons returned and I began to struggle with the knowledge of how I was clinging to my selfish needs. I yearned to live my affective life in a new way, as an expression of something beyond, something bigger and wider than my own little life, but there was a huge resistance within me to let go of old patterns. I slowly became aware, but only in my head, of something about "the first love" and "the second love." Let me explain.

I became more and more intellectually clear that the first love comes from the ultimate life force we call God, who has loved me unconditionally before others knew or loved me. "I have loved you with an everlasting love." And I saw that the second love, the love of parents, family, and friends, was only a modified expression of the first love.

I reasoned that the source of my suffering was the fact that I expected from the second love what only the first love could give. When I hoped for total self-giving and unconditional love from another human being who was imperfect and limited in ability to love, I was asking for the impossible. I knew from experience that the more I demanded, the more others moved away, cut loose, got angry, or left me, and the more I experienced anguish and the pain of rejection. But I felt helpless to change my behavior.

I had never been clear about all this before my time with L'Arche. I always knew that my lifelong struggle was a cry for affection but I didn't realize that I was expecting a first love from those who could only respond with a second love. Clinging to this way of emotional survival at L'Arche Daybreak I sought warm, intimate friendships with people as a way of finding "home." I invested myself in the community and in relationships with people and it worked for a while. During my second year, however, I experienced a very concrete breakage with my best friend. At that moment my whole world came crashing down and it seemed as though all the losses of my whole life came back to haunt me. I completely lost all my bearings as well as my sense of personal integration in Church and community. I cannot express to you how hard it was to suddenly realize that precisely where I had begun to find home, I suddenly discov-

Life may be brimming over with experiences,
but somewhere, deep inside, all of us carry a
vast and fruitful loneliness wherever we go.

From *An Interrupted Life, and Letters From
Westerbork* by Etty Hillesum, 1996, Henry Holt and
Company, New York, p. 93.

ered a profound loneliness and anguish.

I was in agony, shut down, and unable to function. As much as I wanted to work this out in the context of my newfound home, I knew from my training as a psychologist that the community was unable to give me needed professional support and distance to see my situation more clearly. So I left Daybreak to live and come to grips with my struggle in another therapeutic community, in Winnipeg, Manitoba. I was deeply convinced that I was there in order to deepen what it meant for me to be in L'Arche. It was a very, very hard time for me, alone and away from my community while desiring to be there more than ever. This experience would gradually put me in touch with the search for home that was much deeper than friends, intimacy, and safety.

Struggling with this whole thing of having passed from loneliness to L'Arche and now being called from L'Arche to a second loneliness to be able to live in L'Arche, I clearly remembered my first experience of seeing Rembrandt's painting of the prodigal son. I knew then that this painting was to have enormous meaning for my life, and so now, in my solitude in Winnipeg, I began to look at and study the painting for long periods of time.

I'm unable to articulate well what happened to me. I was in so much pain and agony, so utterly lonely, but right there I saw before me this father touching his errant child in a way that was a blessing.

My face is a mask I order to say nothing
About the fragile feelings hiding in my soul.

Glen Lazore (Mohawk).

I identified with the young man and felt how the father touched him with the same affection that I longed for in my heart. That touch of Love was one of recognition by hands, and not so much by eyes or mind but more by heartfelt love. Those hands on my shoulders had something to do with having been known before speech. Living by imagination in the painting moved my grieving heart.

I've been looking at this picture for many years now and it has accompanied me through all the passages I've spoken about: from the loneliness to L'Arche and from L'Arche to the second loneliness, as well as from the second love to the first love. And with my growing awareness, I still believe that this painting holds more for me that is yet to be fully revealed. These insights are in the world of the intellect, but I do believe they help me live the deep emotions of my life.

Primal love, the first unconditional love of the Source of all life, is only reflected to me through limited people: a human mother and father, grandparents, siblings, and mentors. Even though I know that I was knitted together in my mother's womb and totally loved by God, my father was very authoritarian and my mother was terribly scrupulous. Although my parents graced me with enormous love throughout their lives, my initial experiences of the Creator's unconditional love came to me from a nervous, scrupulous woman whose many fears prevented her from freely holding and touching me, and from

Here is the insight most central to spiritual experience: we are known in detail and depth by the love that created and sustains us, known as members of a community of creation that depends on us and on which we depend. This love knows our limits as well as our potential, our capacity for evil as well as good, the persistent self-centeredness with which we exploit the community for our own ends. Yet, as love, it does not seek to confine or manipulate us. Instead, it offers us the constant grace of self-knowledge and acceptance that can liberate us to live a larger love.

From *To Know As We Are Known: Education As a Spiritual Journey* by Parker J. Palmer, 1983, HarperCollins, New York, p. 11.

a father who gave me the strong message that I was to make it in the world and become a professor. God's first unconditional love doesn't radiate too well through two such parents. They were both wonderful people for whom I am eternally grateful, but they were nevertheless broken people and limited people. They loved me with all their ability and they also wounded me. Their love is but a reflection of that unlimited love that already embraced me prior to their knowledge or love of me.

Parental love is a limited reflection of an unlimited love. In the experience of parental love I was wounded as were you, and every other human being. Most parents are the best and the greatest, but in the human experience, parents are also very, very broken people. As much as they desire to give their children the very best, their own brokenness prevents them from being able to do it, and against their own desires they communicate limited love.

Partly for this reason all of us feel the desire to search beyond home for our belovedness, and we generally get caught in many of the cultural movements that exist around us. A dissipated life is one in which we consciously or unconsciously live with the questions "What do you think of me? Look at me! Look at what I'm doing! Look at what I have! Aren't I great? Do you think I'm OK? Do you accept me? Do you see me as good? Do you like me? Do you love me?"

We work tirelessly to present ourselves in a good light before others in the false belief that our identity comes from who we are in *their* eyes, or from what we do or what we have. We look to people outside ourselves to tell us if we are unique, acceptable, and good. We need to know from those around us if we pass the test of being someone unique and lovable. This thinking is encouraged by the world in which we live: How much money does he make? What does she own? Who does he know? Is she famous? What can he do for me? What are they writing about her? Whose arm can he twist? If I don't *do* well or *have* enough money, success, or a good reputation, then I am nothing.

These cultural illusions fill the world in which we live and profoundly influence how we feel about ourselves. They warn us:

> You are what you *do* (lawyer, mother, CEO, teacher, caregiver, scientist, or unskilled laborer), so do something relevant!
>
> You are what you *have* (wealth, education, power, popularity, handicap, nothing), so get busy and acquire all you can!
>
> You are what *others think of you* (kind, mean, saintly, loving, stupid), so act properly and gain respect!

We too often feel that God's love for us is conditional like our love is for others. We have made God in our image rather than seeing ourselves in God's image. . . . Ours is a culture of achievement, and we carry over these attitudes to our relationship with God. We work ourselves to a frazzle trying to impress everyone including God . . . We can believe that our relationship with God, our standing before God, has got nothing to do with our performance, our works.

From *God Has a Dream: A Vision of Hope for Our Times* by Desmond Tutu, 2004, Image Doubleday, New York, p. 32.

Movies, art, and entertainment support these illusions and are forms of manipulation. We are treated endlessly to visions of people who don't know who they are, acting out their dreams for acceptance. We watch as caressing degenerates into grasping, and kissing evolves to biting. Sexual violence follows from the need we have for others to conform to our out-of-control human needs. Seldom is there free giving and receiving but rather we cling to the selfish and possessive expression of our personal needs. The whole area of body and of sexuality is at the center of our search for our true self. That's why we're challenged to gradually move from a dissipated life to a more contained life, not in a prudish way, but because a true identity begets the precious gift of true intimacy.

The life of Jesus refutes this dark world of illusion that entraps us. To return home is to turn from these illusions, from dissipation, and from our desperate attempts to live up to others' expectations. We are not what we do. We are not what we have. We are not what others think of us. Coming home is claiming the truth. I am the beloved child of a loving Creator. We no longer have to beg for permission from the world to exist.

Our choices for a life of either dissipation or containment make a huge difference when it comes to our experience of undeserved suffering. Living our truth in containment allows us to suffer in a whole new way. If, for example, my heart is broken in a relationship, I naturally feel very insecure and I tend to have feelings of low self-esteem and failure as well as hurt and disillusionment. I may want to die, which says much about how I value my life. I have many mixed feelings of the good and the ugly, and my feelings are real. But even when it hurts immensely and I move toward depression, this amazing truth about who I really am remains. I am loved. I know this not because of an intellectual or

I was fired from a job when I was sixteen years old and was devastated. My entire personal worth was laid waste. My mother found me crying in my upstairs room. . . . I told her what happened. . . . She sat down on my bed and took me into her arms. "Fired? Fired?" she laughed. "What the hell is that? Nothing. Tomorrow you'll go looking for another job. That's all." She dabbed at my tears with her handkerchief. ". . . Remember, you were looking for a job when you found the one you just lost. So you'll just be looking for a job one more time." She laughed at her wisdom and my youthful consternation. "And think about it, if you ever get fired again, the boss won't be getting a cherry. You've been through it once, and survived."

From *Wouldn't Take Nothing for My Journey Now* by Maya Angelou, 1993, Random House, New York, p. 80.

psychological experience, but I know it from a place deep within. I am a good person, known and cherished by the One who brought me to my existence. Before I was hurt, I was a beloved. I always have the option, despite my wounded feelings, to turn and reclaim who I really am. This truth about myself that I claim has been constant, a given, since before I was born. I *am* the favored child of a loving Creator.

Jesus knew who he was and was thus able to live the days of his passion in agony and peace. He didn't need to blame others or himself, because he understood the brokenness of those who caused him pain. Jesus, in the knowledge that he was loved, was able to stand in his pain and forgive those who wounded him.

For me the experience of homecoming is around my deep need for affection, which expresses itself in many ways in my heart and body. This human longing often projects me into the world of fantasy where yearning, loneliness, lust, anger, hurt, and revenge overwhelm me. Because of what I know to be true, and in the midst of my pain, I may reflect, "Right here is my opportunity to return. Right at this point I can gently turn back to the truth. I haven't come home yet. Yes, I have a body and my body is good and I can touch people and be touched. But I have to touch and be touched from the place of my belovedness more than from the place of my need."

Jesus said, "As the Father loves me, so I also love you." Clinging to the knowledge of being first of all a beloved son who is not fully home yet holds me from slipping into a life of total dissipation. I may not yet be fully contained, but that doesn't change the fact that my body is a temple where the creative Spirit resides. It doesn't change the fact that, like Jesus, I am a beloved son of God. That is the truth.

A contained life is returning to and living this primal truth. It's a real struggle to bring our whole selves home and it is best accomplished gently and gradually. Jesus tells us it is a narrow path, meaning that we slip off occasionally, and that is OK. The whole course of the spiritual life is falling off, and returning, slipping away from the truth and turning back to it, leaving and returning. So in our leaving, as much as in our returning, we must try to remember that we are blessed, loved, cherished, and waited for by the One whose love doesn't change.

Dear Child of God, in our world it is often hard to remember that God loves you just as you are. God loves you not because you are good. No, God loves you, period. God loves us not because we are lovable. No, we are lovable precisely because God loves us. It is marvellous when you come to understand that you are accepted for who you are, apart from any achievement. It is so liberating.

From *God Has a Dream: A Vision of Hope for Our Time* by Desmond Tutu, 2004, Image Doubleday, New York, pp. 31–32.

Loving our incarnate selves, body and heart, is all about homecoming. It is the gathering of everything into oneness. As body, mind, and heart become one, the dissipation falls away and we feel more whole, more contained, more one with self and the universe. It is from there we tenderly touch another, embrace her, wash and care for his body, hold her, love him, kiss her, and feel free. In that place we no longer need the other to tell us who we are or to give us an identity. Like Jesus, we know who we are, children forever loved by our personal God.

When you go back to South Africa and stand up to preach and teach, remember always that each person sits next to their own pool of tears.

From *Listening to the Ground* by Trevor Hudson, 2007, Upper Room Books.

Returning, then, is moving toward containment, toward home, holding fast to our true identity as the beloved of Love Divine. We might know it with our minds, but our bodies often take us by another way, running around out of control and all over the place. The spiritual life is a life in which we continually turn toward the truth, toward home, and hopefully those who love us help us turn back to ourselves, as the favored daughters or sons of the Spirit of Love.

My crisis with my friend precipitated my entry into a new loneliness unlike my former loneliness at Harvard and Yale. This second loneliness was much more radical and existential; something about going beyond the interpersonal into the mystical, and trusting that by giving over my specific attachment and need for my friend, something larger would be given. It was really about the Divine becoming the center of my life. It had to do with Jesus' invitation in Scripture, "Leave your father, leave your mother, leave your brother, leave your sister, leave your friends, and you will have a hundred brothers, and sisters, and friends." I must dare to speak of it because "the second loneliness" is a contemporary way to describe the oldest mystical traditions about the spiritual life. The dark night of the soul is another image of the second loneliness. In the experience of the dark night, Saint John of the Cross gradually understood that the Spirit will never be owned or grasped in the affections of the human heart because God's Spirit is so much greater than our human capacity.

My most profound learning from this time was about the passage from that first loneliness of emotionally unsatisfying friendships to the second loneliness of a demanding intimacy with Love Itself. This deeper communion with God did not invite me to renounce friendship altogether, but it challenged me to let go of certain emotional, intellec-

The first call is frequently to follow Jesus or to prepare ourselves to do wonderful and noble things for the Kingdom. We are appreciated and admired by family, by friends, or by the community. The second call comes later, when we accept that we cannot do big or heroic things for Jesus; it is a time of renunciation, humiliation, and humility.

From *Community and Growth* by Jean Vanier, 1979, Darton, Longman, and Todd, London, p. 139.

tual, and affective satisfactions. This second loneliness is not something for me to overcome but to live, standing up and as a full human being. This second loneliness is one that sets me interiorly on the road to communion with the Divine and at the same time brings me in touch with my deepest self in relationship with brothers, sisters, and good friends.

It is paradoxical but real. The more I find intimacy with the Creator of my life, the more loneliness I experience. And at the very same time this loneliness offers me a new sense of belonging to the family of Divine Love that is much greater and more intimate than any belonging that the world can offer. The world of communion with the Great Spirit that is truly experienced as a world of loneliness and the highest level of separation from my human yearning to be loved, is also revealed to me as the highest level of belonging to the Creator of the galaxies and being part of the human race.

In the deeps are the violence and terror of which psychology has warned us. But if you ride these monsters down, if you drop with them farther over the world's rim, you find what our sciences cannot locate or name, the substrate, the ocean or matrix or ether which buoys the rest, which gives goodness its power for good, and evil its power of evil, the unified field: our complex and inexplicable caring for each other, and for our life together here. This is given. It is not learned.

From *Teaching a Stone to Talk* by Annie Dillard, 1982, HarperCollins, New York, pp. 94–95.

In the second loneliness, the greatest loneliness and the greatest solidarity with the Divine Lover and with the human condition are coming together. Once I accept this passage as a call to be deeply, deeply connected with Unconditional Love, with my own fragile humanity, and with brothers and sisters everywhere, something shifts within. Allowing God's first love to be primary for me changes the way I live my existential loneliness, mainly because I am more rooted in the truth, and thus more able to live my suffering while standing as a full, human person.

This is the reason I suggested earlier that we not enter the story of the prodigal son alone, but rather bring others with us into it. Each of us is conscious that we are surrounded by a lonely, suffering world of people. If we are to touch our own, unique second loneliness, we need to be in touch with the larger picture of the human condition of which we are part. So, once again, let me ask you to try to see yourself and your unique life as one that is in solidarity with many others in the world. Otherwise your life remains small, isolated, uninteresting. You and I, in our limited communities of family and church, are broken, little people. Somehow, with our more scientific and cosmic worldview, we are invited to break through to a broader communion with others in the world and with the holy One of the universe.

If I encourage you to live the great struggle of your life and your pain standing up, I do so trusting that we are in solidarity with something larger than our individuality. Mary stood under the Cross. *Stabat mater* is the Latin for "the standing mother." Under the Cross she didn't faint but stood with her son and with the world in her suffering. I confess to you that I cannot fully do it, but I know for sure that I'm called to stand, to look upon the world and proclaim what our humanity is really about. We are very small and little—that's the mystery. Hopefully my personal experience and the many reflections that follow in this book will generate in you the desire to make your own personal connection with the Gospel story.

I remember the day a young engineer came to me and said, "Henri, something really powerful happened to me. I was driving on the highway in a car and I felt terribly lonely and then an inner voice, perhaps the voice of Jesus, seemed to say to me, 'Why don't you take this dirt road, then step out of your car, and we'll walk together.' So I left my car behind and I was feeling very alone. I tried to imagine that Jesus and I were walking together, but I felt incredibly lonely. At the very same moment I knew that he was speaking to me in my heart. And I also knew in a flash that I was closer to him than ever before. It's hard to explain but that encounter was so real for me. I know I'll never be the same because of it."

This little story reminds me of how a human life is a life that moves from the first loneliness of driving on the highway in alienation to the second loneliness of walking alone with Jesus, trusting that He is enough. Unmet needs continue to scream from within but we no longer demand healing from lovers and friends.

My life in L'Arche became the way for me to encounter the central struggle of my life, namely the second loneliness revealed to me by experience and by the parable of the prodigal son. Through them I've touched God's first, unconditional love. The story and the painting reveal to me that it is possible to experience goodness, friendship, and affection without my whole life becoming dependent upon it. It is also possible to feel rejected and abandoned without being destroyed. There's nothing as painful as being rejected, but if it is lived against the background of the first love, it becomes possible to survive. This is a story of the spiritual life.

As a hart longs for flowing streams,
so longs my soul for You
O Beloved.
My soul thirsts for the Beloved,
for the Living Water.
When may I come and behold
your face?
Tears have been my only nourishment
day and night
While friends ask continually,
"Where is the Beloved of your
heart?"

From *Psalms for Praying* by Nan C. Merrill, 1996, The Continuum International Publishing Group, New York, Psalm 42, p. 81.

Look closely at Rembrandt's painting and study it, alone and with other spiritual searchers like yourself. Try to grasp that this practically blind father, who recognizes his beloved child not so much by seeing as by touching, has something very primal to do with real human loving and being loved. It has nothing to do with declarations or statements or arguments. The father's love is before speech. This intimate connection with unconditional love sends us back to our very first experience of being loved by the way we were touched. The initial touch by Divine Love and by our parents entered into our consciousness and offered us our first sense of being loved uniquely, and it gave us our first experience of home, of belonging, of safety and protection. Throughout our lives it seems we continue to yearn for that first touch that reassured us that we were indeed beloved.

As I've "lived" these past years with the painting, I read hundreds of exegetical stories about it. The variations of people's interpretations, from the most sociological to the most intimate, are legion, and some of them boggle the imagination. Because it is so open-ended, this is one of the greatest stories in the Gospel and in literature as a

It doesn't interest me what you do for a living. I want to know what you ache for, and if you dare to dream of meeting your heart's longing. . . . I want to know if you will risk looking like a fool for love, for your dream, for the adventure of being alive. . . . I want to know if you have touched the center of your own sorrow, if you have been opened by life's betrayals or have become shrivelled and closed from fear of further pain. I want to know if you can sit with pain, mine or your own, without moving to hide it or fade it or fix it. . . . I want to know if you can disappoint another to be true to yourself.

From *The Invitation* by Oriah Mountain Dreamer, 1999, HarperSanFrancisco, San Francisco, p. 1.

whole. That's encouraging because it implies that each one of us is also free to make our own exegesis. I'm trying to explain mine in what I've already written about my experience, and that's also why my comments about the prodigal son have a lot to do with me. But the beauty is that there is meaning for your life and your story, too, because every human life has its own exegetical possibilities. Your life is profoundly important, so I beg you to take yourself very seriously in the light of this exegetical story that has meaning for your most intimate human journey.

Listening

Become still. Listen to the hearts of the people in the parable and become conscious of their loneliness. Move slowly back to the painting, asking for new eyes to see and new ears to hear the heart-cries of each one. Look and listen with your heart and feel their individual pain. Perhaps their loneliness reaches into yours. In this sacred context don't be afraid to give yourself time to feel your own existential loneliness as a full member of the human family.

Journaling

With pen in hand, attempt to translate your thoughts and feelings into words for your journal. Move deeply into your heart and write of your experiences of loneliness in relationships and in the absence of relationships. How does loneliness affect your sense of yourself? Dare to express yourself and don't stop until you do. Finish by expressing how the story and the painting give light to your precious life.

Communing

Imagine yourself in the very presence of your loving Creator and let your heart speak. Name your aloneness and your struggle to find love, to give love, and to love yourself. Honestly identify yourself as a victim of not having been loved perfectly, and ask for help to reclaim your lovableness. Honestly identify how you have wounded others, and with confidence ask pardon. Express your heartfelt longing to rest secure again in the embrace of the One who loves you with an everlasting love. Be still, and listen for the response.

Heart speaks to heart.

The word humility, like the human, comes from humas, *or earth. We are most human when we do no great things. We are not so important; we are simply dust and spirit—at best, loving midwives, participants in a process much larger than we. If we are quiet and listen and feel how things move, perhaps we will be wise enough to put our hands on what waits to be born, and bless it with kindness and care.*

From *Sabbath: Restoring the Sacred Rhythm of Rest* by Wayne Muller, 1999, Bantam Books, New York, p. 176.

A Wisdom Practice for Those on a Spiritual Journey

Practice #3   CLAIM YOUR TRUE IDENTITY

The whole parable is about the journey of an arrogant, lost, and set-free adolescent finding the path to mature adulthood. He thinks he knows the way to unlimited pleasure but gets painfully lost along the way. The story ends as he falteringly "claims" his true belonging and "tastes" the truth of who he really is—a beloved child.

Personally, as my struggle reveals, I don't often "feel" like a beloved child of God. But I *know* that that is my most primal identity and I know that I must choose it above and beyond my hesitations.

Strong emotions, self-rejection, and even self-hatred justifiably toss you about, but you are free to respond as you will. You are *not* what others, or even you, think about yourself. You are *not* what you do. You are *not* what you have. You are a full member of the human family, having been known before you were conceived and molded in your mother's womb. In times when you feel bad about yourself, try to choose to remain true to the truth of who you really are. Look in the mirror each day and claim your true identity. Act ahead of your feelings and trust that one day your feelings will match your convictions. Choose now and continue to choose this incredible truth. As a spiritual practice claim and reclaim your primal identity as beloved daughter or son of a personal Creator.

part two

The Invisible Exile of Resentment

4

the elder son

As I said earlier, I knew that besides the runaway, there was also an elder son in me that needed to return home. It is my belief that the eldest in the story of the prodigal son is the figure standing to the right of the father in the painting. Once again I invite you to situate yourself in the small center where you live your unique life, with all your family, friends, brothers, and sisters on the planet around you. Now listening from your deepest heart, journey with me into the story of the other sibling as paraphrased from the parable. (The full text is in Luke 15:11–32.)

The elder son, returning from his work in the fields, heard a commotion.

When he inquired, one of the servants told him, "Your brother is home, safe and sound. Your father has killed the fatted calf and ordered a celebration."

When we listen to a sentence, a story, or a parable not simply to be instructed, informed, or inspired but to be formed into a truly obedient person, then the Book offers trustworthy spiritual insight. The daily practice of lectio divina (sacred reading), over time, transforms our personal identity, our actions, and our common life of faith. . . . Scripture does have a personal word for us, yet knowledge of historic Christian teaching helps us avoid the easy trap of wanting scripture to support our own designs.

From *Spiritual Direction: Wisdom for the Long Walk of Faith* by Henri J. M. Nouwen, 2006, HarperSanFrancisco, San Francisco, p. xviii.

The elder son was angry and refused to go in.

His father came out and urged him to attend the feast.

But the young man retorted, "All these years I have slaved for you and never once disobeyed you. Yet you never offered me so much as a kid for me to celebrate with my friends. Now, for this son of yours, coming home after swallowing up your property—he and his loose women—you kill the fatted calf?"

The father responded, "My son, you have always been with me. All I have is yours. And it is also right to celebrate and rejoice, because your brother was dead, and has come to life. He was lost and is found."

I'm happy to reflect with you what I'm learning about the elder son and all he represents for us in our own lives. His most visible characteristic is that he did not run away but stayed home. Consider this carefully. This young person is the one who, from an objective perspective, did everything right. He did not take off, but rather he worked hard and took care of his father's estate. He was obedient and dutiful, committed and faithful. It is obvious that the gift of the eldest was his faithfulness. The father relied on him and on his steady, hard work to keep the estate going. Undoubtedly, because of this work, the family prospered.

However, all was not as perfect as it seemed. I say this because even though he did stay home, it is apparent that he had wandered far away in his mind and heart. Listen carefully to his words: "All these years I have slaved for you and never once disobeyed any of your orders. And yet you never offered me so much as a kid for me to celebrate with my friends." Hear his "earning" as opposed to "intimacy" mentality. Hear his bitterness and resentment.

This was not a happy young man. He harbored dark feelings as well as angry thoughts about the one in the family who had grabbed the inheritance and run off to satisfy selfish desires. We quickly see that the faithfulness of this stay-at-home adult child wasn't entirely pure. On the contrary it was loaded. I can imagine his inner monologue directed toward his father: "Why on earth would you give that

You don't choose your family. They are God's gift to you, as you are to them. Perhaps if we could we might have chosen different brothers and sisters. Fortunately or unfortunately we can't. We have them as they have us. And no matter how your brother may be, you can't renounce him. . . . Can you imagine what would happen in this world if we accepted that fact about ourselves—that whether we like it or not we are members of one family?

From God Has a Dream: A Vision of Hope for Our Time by Desmond Tutu, 2004, Doubleday, New York, p. 22.

worthless good-for-nothing so much of *our* money? How could you bow to such arrogance and disrespect? Don't you even 'get it' that he's a loser? Can't you appreciate that I am here working my head off for you while he goes out and does all those despicable things? Why should I have to stay and work while he spends our money to dissipate himself? You have no expectations of him, whereas you and everyone else *expect* me to be dutiful."

It is interesting to note right here how the younger son got lost in quite a spectacular way. He was completely open about his desire to move far away into a dissipated lifestyle of greed and lust, having his women, gambling, and finally losing everything including himself. His departure implies that he knew he was lost and so did everybody else! And in the end, he was also overt about his return home. He seemed unashamed about his choices and felt no need to hide his adulterous lifestyle. Family image and a good reputation weren't priorities for him.

On the other hand, the elder son's story that looks so righteous on the surface was far from peaceful. Yes, he *was* obedient, but his actions were tempered with reticence, and without any real interaction with his father. His relationship to his father showed no signs of being free or flowing, nor was it really safe either. Listen very carefully to his words about his younger brother: "This son of yours who lived a loose life with those women." He doesn't say, "my brother." He says, "this son of yours."

And the father answers, "Your brother has returned."

Note how one of the characteristics of the elder's resentment is separation from any identification with his younger sibling. He is not even close to accepting his brother as his own flesh and blood, nor as the one with whom he grew up, played, and shared a significant history. No, he's inwardly raging with anger and judgment: "that son of yours. *I* am not that way. *He* is that way. And yet you throw *him* a big party and invite lots of people, but *I* do all the hard work around here. All our other siblings with their families and friends will arrive and party and have a wonderful day without ever knowing how much *I* had to do to make the whole party possible. After they talk and party they'll leave the place in a mess and *I'll* do the clean-up, because *I'm* the one who's responsible for it all."

The father did not react to the darkness in his eldest son but rather approached him in a spirit of collaboration for the building up of the estate over many years. "All that is mine is yours," says his father. There is a wonderful intimacy here, an affection and gratitude

Rembrandt sensed the deepest meaning of this when he painted the elder son at the side of the platform where the younger son is received in the father's joy. He didn't depict the celebration, with its musicians and dancers; they were merely the external signs of the father's joy. . . . In place of the party, Rembrandt painted light, the radiant light that envelops both father and son. The joy that Rembrandt portrays is the still joy that belongs to God's house. . . . The elder son stands outside the circle of this love, refusing to enter. The light on his face makes it clear that he, too, is called to the light, but he cannot be forced.

From *The Return of the Prodigal Son: A Story of Homecoming* by Henri J. M. Nouwen, 1992, Doubleday, New York, p. 69.

on the part of the father for his eldest son. Of course it was difficult for the young man to stay in the family home, but being there was also an opportunity for him to cooperate with his father and to become an equal player in carrying responsibility. Surely there were differences between the two of them. Like life, it wasn't simple, but the partnership held potential for growth and fulfillment at the same time. Instead, this son looked away from his privileged partnership, gave resentment a place in his heart, and was less and less able to situate himself uniquely in the family. No wonder he was unable to celebrate his brother's return!

Resentment is one of the most pervasive evils of our time. Resentment is rampant in our society. Resentment is very pernicious and very, very destructive, and you and I are seldom free from it.

I know a really wonderful teacher who's done wonders with some of the children she's taught. She's experienced, dedicated, and excellent in the classroom. In any setting with peers, however, she's the one who is always busy, always doing for others, and always fussing about details around the gathering. It's clear that she doesn't feel comfortable as part of a circle of equals. This lady transforms every social situation into a job by bustling about in the group, helping people with their coats, seeing that everyone has something to eat or drink, tidying up, doing the dishes, but never taking time to really be relaxed and present to others or enjoy herself. I hear people say of her, "She's so good, always sacrificing herself and helping get things done!" The difficulty is that that kind of affirmation never allows her to become aware that she is being praised for actions that stem from not feeling equal to others in the group, and possibly from deep-seated resentment.

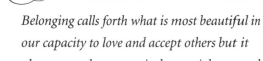

Resentment, the curse of the faithful, the virtuous, the obedient, and the hardworking, settles itself in the human heart and causes havoc. That is why it's important to think and reflect upon it. All of us who give our lives for loved ones, work hard, and objectively have many virtues to be praised, are sometimes not really free from the burden of resentment in our hearts.

Belonging calls forth what is most beautiful in our capacity to love and accept others but it also can awaken anger, jealousy, violence, and the refusal to cooperate.

From *Becoming Human* by Jean Vanier, 1998, House of Anansi Press, Toronto, p. 58.

Each of us knows anger, and anger is real. We are powerless to simply turn it off and it fills our inner space with added distress. So, what can we do about our anger? Psychology tells us that if we are in touch with our angry feelings, name them, and even perhaps lash out, the anger loses some of its power over us. We are encouraged to "work with" our anger, enter into our reasons for being upset, and try to engage with those who wound us. "Damn it! I'm furious with you! But I beg you to talk with me about what has happened. Should we invite someone to help us talk to each other? How can we come to terms with this upset so we can each get on with our lives?" This type of action prevents resentment from building a home in our hearts.

But when, in our efforts to be pious, we eat up the angry feelings and do not make them known, resentment begins. One begins feeling a little angry but does nothing about it. With time, as unattended anger builds in a given relationship or life situation, one becomes progressively more irate. The constant swallowing of negative feelings causes them to pervade the inner universe and usurp one's power to relate in a truly loving way. Gradually it is no longer hot anger, but it grows cold and settles itself deep into the innermost heart. And over the long term, resentment becomes a way of being.

Resentment is cold anger. That's what it is. The greatest difficulty with resentment is that it's very hidden and interior as opposed to being overt. It has the potential to present itself as holiness and that makes it even more pernicious. Resentment resides in the very depths of our hearts, sitting in our bones and our flesh while we are mostly unaware of its presence. Whereas we might imagine that we are faithful and good, we may in fact be very lost in a much deeper way than someone who is overtly acting out. The

A brother who was insulted by another brother came to Abba Sisoes, and said to him: "I was hurt by my brother and I want to avenge myself."

The old man tried to console him and said: "Don't do that, my child. Rather leave vengeance to God."

But he said: "I will not quit until I avenge myself."

Then the old man said: "Let us pray, brother"; and standing up, he said, "O God, we no longer need you to take care of us since we now avenge ourselves."

Hearing these words, the brother fell at the feet of the old man and said: "I am not going to fight with my brother anymore. Forgive me, Abba."

From *Desert Wisdom,* by Yushi Nomura, ed., 1982, Orbis Books, Maryknoll, NY, p. 53.

younger son in the story goes out, makes a fool of himself, and then returns. That's a very clear-cut movement. But the resentful person objectively never gets lost in the first place, so what does returning look like for such a one? Perhaps it is much harder to heal from resentment than from dissipation.

The elder son epitomizes something important in his response to his life situation. Without appreciation for his good fortune and the promise of a secure future as overseer of the land, he's basically a frustrated, angry, and unhappy young man. He's oblivious to the fact that he probably feels insecure outside the safety of his own home. In the harshness of his judgments, he's not conscious that he probably would be threatened to face his father and ask for money to travel and see the world. He's blind to the way in which he stayed home, worked hard, and acted politely enough, but without his heart being engaged. And he's probably the only one who hasn't recognized his frozen smile as a cover-up for the anger that seeps out in all his interactions.

So the one in the story who in many respects did the objectively good thing, the person who was praised as the "good son" as compared with the "bad one," the one who stayed home, worked hard, was obedient to the old father, and was faithful, ended up being as lost spiritually as the younger guy who ran off and dissipated his inheritance. But the elder was lost in a very different and complex way. Unlike the dissipation of the younger, the elder was far away from home emotionally because of resentment.

What would constitute his return? What if he experienced a breakthrough and on the other hand said, "I'm so glad I was always obe-

Where do people find the courage to live divided no more . . . ? In the Rosa Parks story, that insight emerges in a wonderful way. After she had sat at the front of the bus for a while, the police came aboard and said, "You know, if you continue to sit there, we're going to have to throw you in jail." Rosa Parks replied, "You may do that . . ." which is a very polite way of saying, "What could your jail of stone and steel possibly mean to me, compared to the self-imposed imprisonment I've suffered for forty years—the prison I've just walked out of by refusing to conspire any longer with this racist system?"

From *Let Your Life Speak: Listening for the Voice of Vocation* by Parker J. Palmer, 2000, Jossey-Bass, San Francisco, p. 34.

dient and I listened to you, and never once disobeyed your wishes. It's been hard but I've learned so much and I recognize how fruitful our collaboration has been." I can only imagine how differently he would approach his life. When the story ends, it seems that he remains full of angry virtue, but there is always hope of his possible return.

Listening

In your quiet space take a moment to inhale outer and inner silence, while you exhale outer and inner noise. Gradually focus your attention on the elder son in the parable. Listen to what you are thinking when you look at him. What do his words and his silence say to you? Consider if the bitterness in his heart touches something in yours. Converse with him and discover how he thinks and feels. Listen and be open to the ways that you and he are alike.

Journaling

Begin by listing everything in Rembrandt's painting that distinguishes the elder sibling from the others in the parable. Pause. Now venture back into Chapter Four and complete your list with any other insights about him that are there. Pause again. Next, slowly reread the list, point by point, from the position of *your* hidden, inner life. Begin to list the characteristics about yourself that mirror his. Dare to confront yourself in honesty, unarmed and unafraid of your truth. Write what you see in yourself and how you feel about what you see.

Communing

Surrender. Speak slowly of all you have written to the Presence of Love that is with you. Point by point give everything into the hands that hold you. Offer your thanks for what you are learning about yourself and

A period of rest . . . is a spiritual and biological necessity. A lack of dormancy produces confusion and erosion in the life force.

From *Sabbath: Restoring the Sacred Rhythm of Rest* by Wayne Muller, 1999, Bantam Books, New York, p. 7.

about being loved without having to earn it. Ask for the strength to become more aware of the hidden exile of your self-righteousness and judgments. Ask for wisdom and courage. Listen for the response.

Heart speaks to heart.

Practice #4 LOVE THOSE WHO ARE DIFFERENT

Prevented by resentment from any identification with his younger sibling, the firstborn son indignantly refers his father to "That son of yours . . ." The loving father, without judging either child, gently reminds the elder of his important connection with the younger:

> Your *brother* was lost.

I'm getting the message that I'm a beloved child so it's time for me to stop offering friendship to my friends and withholding love from my "enemies." Now I want to recognize many real sisters and brothers from the place of my own acting shamefully and also leaving home. I want to grow in likeness to the father figure in the parable.

Jesus teaches us in the Sermon on the Mount, "Love your enemies." Rationally that makes no sense at all since the enemy is, by definition, the one that we do not love. But Jesus not only spoke this wisdom. He lived it. As disciples, we try to follow his teaching and see ourselves as brothers and sisters in the human family, no better and no worse than any other person. Let us look at the life of Jesus and learn the meaning of his teachings about difficult relationships.

> Do good to those who hate you, bless those who curse you, and pray for those who treat you badly.

Treat others as you would like people to treat you.

If you love those who love you, what credit can you expect? Even sinners love those who love them.

Instead, love your enemies, and do good to them, and lend without any hope of return. You will have great reward, and you will be children of the Most High.

God is kind to the ungrateful and the wicked.

(LUKE 6)

the hidden exile of resentment

Once, in talking about the parable to a friend, I was confiding how I sometimes felt a desperate urge to run away to a life of self-indulgence and freedom from commitments. I confessed how, like the prodigal, I longed to break free from places of being known and go off to a foreign land where I could indulge myself and let loose.

I remember my friend looking at me and saying with great compassion, "Henri, it may be that you think your problem is that

Abba Poemen said:

"There is one sort of person

who seems to be silent,

but inwardly criticizes other people.

Such a person is really talking all the time."

From *Desert Wisdom* by Yushi Nomura, ed., 1982, Orbis Books, Maryknoll, NY, p. 83.

of the young runaway in the story, but I'm sitting here listening to you and wondering if you aren't much more like the elder son rather than the younger!" I was shocked! In all my reading of the story I had hardly noticed the elder brother and had never once considered any identification with him as a possibility. But that observation by my friend opened a door for me and allowed me to touch a whole different set of questions from the point of view of the one who was obedient, dutiful, and the eldest in the family. My process of identifying with this person in the story has truly become a source of new, important, and painful memories as well as connections with my own life, beginning in my family of origin.

My own father was one of eleven children, all of whom got married but one. As in many families at that time, there were named or unnamed expectations on the unmarried daughter, the one who stayed home. I can still hear my aunt reiterating how she was giving her life to take care of her aging mother, and I recognized that that was an honorable thing to do. However, it seemed to me as though she wasn't enjoying herself. I know now that she was a very intelligent and articulate woman, and I feel that she had many reasons to be angry. I also believe that she interiorized her anger, eating it up more and more as time went on. Externally she tried to be sweet about it, but meanwhile most of us could see that she wasn't feeling well. Resentment grew in her because in those days there were few ways for her to express herself or to be helped in her lonely journey. All of us knew but no one asked or provided an opening for her to explode, "Yes, I feel used and abused, and furthermore I'm as angry as hell. You people are busy and fulfilled and you never really listen to *me*. Did you ever imagine how hard my life is and how tired I am? Are you aware that I have no privacy and no life of my own? Can you not see that I'm exhausted, upset, frustrated, and angry?"

On the one hand my aunt was generous, but on the other hand her sacrifice was so enormous that she eventually suffered from a buildup of resentment inside. She *was* giving her whole life and we all knew she was determined to do it until her mother died. I remember hearing family members say, "Look how Aunt Clara is doing it all. Isn't that wonderful?" She *was* fulfilling family expectations, but she was also feeling desperate and isolated with her lot in life. I believe she wasn't free or able to find people to help her deal with her lack of freedom and her feelings of being used. Whereas I used to look at my aunt with scorn, today I feel a deep compassion for her and for all she lived in those years with my grandmother.

Furthermore, I personally identify with her as I also identify with this elder brother in the story because I recognize how, over time, there has been a buildup of resentment in me. I am the oldest in our family and I suspect that since my time in university resentment has claimed a piece of my heart, espe-

The artistry of the trapeze troupe emerges from a cooperative effort to create something of fleeting and fragile beauty. It knows danger but not violence, courage but not conquest, striving for excellence but not competition, the joy of achievement but not victory.

From *Learning to Fly: Reflections on Fear, Trust, and the Joy of Letting Go* by Sam Kean, 1999, Broadway Books, New York.

cially in my relationship with my dad. You see, he accomplished his goals late in life by becoming a successful professor of law, and based on his background this rise to fame was quite unusual in his day. My dad was very bright and able to function well in the world of competition. I, as the oldest in our family, seemed to be programmed to believe that I had to be at least as good as my dad. Thus began a sort of lifelong competition with respect to our careers and to most other subjects as well. When I started to study for the priesthood, he began to read theology. Then, when I went into psychology, he began to acquaint himself with that discipline. I felt by the way that he questioned and challenged me, he was vying with me to have the last word on the subject. On the one hand my father was a very loving person, but on the other hand it was as if he most often responded to me with "I could have told you that long ago!" This observation was unique between my father and me and made me frustrated, especially because it wasn't like that between him and my other siblings. I often felt angry, but I swallowed it and never spoke about it to anyone. Today I can speak of it, but while I was in it, I kept it to myself because that is what I thought I should do. It didn't fill my consciousness but the relationship between us wasn't free and flowing either, and I know now that resentment was at work in me.

I also know that since I was a child my heart has consistently yearned for intimacy, and I've always lived as though I had to earn it. Failing to claim so much of what I desired that was actually abundantly present to me, I worked hard to prove myself deserving of the love that I felt I needed to live. So in many respects I identify strongly with the experience of the elder son's work-to-earn-love patterns.

Abba Mios was asked by a soldier whether God would forgive a sinner. After instructing him at some length, the old man asked him: "Tell me, my dear, if your cloak were torn, would you throw it away?" "Oh no!" he replied, "I would mend it and wear it again." The old man said to him: "Well, if you care for your cloak, will not God show mercy to his own creature?"

From *Desert Wisdom* by Yushi Nomura, ed., 1982, Orbis Books, Maryknoll, NY, p. 11.

When the time came to leave home I happily departed, but I also very consciously took the time to stay connected, be obedient to my parents' expectations, and be sure that the family remained as one of my priorities. I was choosing to do what was *right* and that is why I understand this resentful mentality. My younger siblings were entirely different from me. They left home to pursue their goals with much more freedom than me. At one point one brother went into an incredible crisis, and he did something that I never could have done. He just let it all fall apart right in front of our father. I remember how fully he shared everything with my dad, everything in a most devastating crisis. And there the two of them sat, loving each other with enormous intimacy like two brothers. My dad spoke so lovingly about him, and seemed to have no need to compete with him at all, ever. You can imagine that I had a hard time with that, but because I was pious, I simply ate it up and never dealt with it. Now I can say that my faithfulness wasn't free and had little to do with piety. Despite my angst, I clung to this safe way of looking good and being unfree in my ability to relate easily. Besides that I harbored jealous and bitter feelings toward my siblings' ability to act with much more freedom than me, and that had a profound impact on the way I related with them. Only now I realize that I can't change that past, but I can respect the individual histories and claim my own freedom in response to my family now.

I offer this personal struggle simply to demonstrate how hard it was for me to trust my unique place as the eldest son in my family. I seem to have lived my life convincing myself that the work-to-earn-love ethic is what a good life looks like. However, this image for my life has been consistently interrupted, and my ideals torn to shreds. I hear myself complaining, "Why is it that all those damn things keep happening within and around me and I can't live my ideal?" Personal failure, family tragedy, financial struggles, historical disasters, and political disillusionments have each, in time, interrupted my ideal life and caused me grief. Meanwhile, over the course of all these disillusionments, I continued to eat up the anger and allowed resentment to find a perfect home in my heart.

My friend inviting me to focus on the elder sibling led me to the realization that this person lives inside of me, so I understand his experience from within. The eldest child in the parable believed that he had to earn his father's love. "I've done this for you and I've done that, and you haven't recognized me. You haven't given me anything in return." He sees himself in relationship to his father as a boss is with a worker or slave. I also assumed his twisted logic and I know that in doing so I wounded my father and prompted his angry sentiments. "Really, were you expecting a little present from me to prove to you

Thank you, Lord, for the gift of my life thus far. Thank you for your teaching in this parable that opens me to new possibilities for my own life. Send me your loving Spirit of Wisdom to help me listen and identify my resentments with those of the elder son. Show me the signs of my hidden exile from fulfillment because of my self-righteousness and judgments. Help me to not be afraid to seriously consider what I can do about my angers and my fears. I desire to grow in love and acceptance of all my brothers and sisters, as well as of myself, as I am. But I need wisdom, strength, and courage. Please come to me and remain close to me.

From the tapes of Henri Nouwen's workshop.

that I love you? Why don't you look at me and trust that I rejoiced in your coming before you were even born? Don't you know that I recognize you as my flesh and blood, that I know you well, and that I love you deeply? Can't you even see that my love has nothing to do with whether you work hard or not? Whether you stay home or not, act faithfully or not, slave for me or not? I love you because you are my firstborn child. You don't have to earn points with me and afterward be rewarded by having a little party. The thought that you have to deserve being my son wounds me. You *are* my son and I love you!"

Strange how the need to earn love dies hard in me, even though the more I cling to it, the harder it is for me to live my life journey without bitterness. I can't seem to stop working hard to prove something and then search for a rationale that will help me understand "Why do they treat me like that?" or "What more can I do to prove that I deserve more?" or "Why do I have to work so hard to be in this relationship?" I simply don't understand why people don't appreciate how hard I'm trying to be worthy.

My identification with the elder son has made me aware of the enormous spiritual difference between working my whole life long to earn the equality, love, and friendship that I need in my primary relationships and of living these relationships out of gratitude for the boundless, gratuitous gifts that continuously shower down upon me in my life. In the former, my refusal to accept that I am already lovable destroys trust and corrodes my heart, while in the latter, my difficulties become opportunities to trust

Reading often means gathering information, acquiring new insight and knowledge, and mastering a new field. It can lead us to degrees, diplomas, and certificates. Spiritual reading however, is different. It means not simply reading about spiritual things but also reading about spiritual things in a spiritual way. . . . As we read spiritually about spiritual things, we open our hearts to God's voice. Sometimes we must be willing to put down the book we are reading and just listen to what God is saying to us through its words.

From *Bread for the Journey: A Daybook of Wisdom and Faith* by Henri J. M. Nouwen, 1997, HarperSanFrancisco, San Francisco, entry for April 15.

even more that love will carry me toward my mature humanity. I have the ability to respond to my relational difficulties from two points of view and I must choose my direction. Either I say, "Watch me, God, and see how much I'm working for you. Don't you think you should finally love me?" or I say, "Oh loving Creator, thank you for gifting me with life and with unconditional love. Help me to continuously be grateful for your generosity and trust that you are always with me to help me to love." Either I am the victim of others' cruelty or my pain is the impetus for my transformation. This distinction and my freedom to respond shape the unfolding of my spiritual life. Choosing to act from the love that is always present with me in my suffering I become grounded in my identity as a beloved son of God. This is the path to greater and greater freedom and intimacy with the first love, the One who chose me before I was born.

Earlier in this work I reflected with you about the distinction between the first love and all other loves in the spiritual life. At this point in my spiritual journey I choose to claim the first love, independent of what I do, what I have, or what others think of me. I am a beloved son of God who was loved since before time began. Claiming this truth is the inner work that I commit to today and it leads me to see that I must respond to life's interruptions from a new perspective. It is radical for me, involving an almost constant effort to overcome my resistance to old patterns. That is why I have resolved to give time to reflect on this invitation, to pray often in gratitude and petition, and to find the necessary support and accountability for my commitment.

I have learned through bitter experience the one supreme lesson to conserve my anger, and as heat conserved is transmuted into energy, even so our anger controlled can be transmuted into a power which can move the world.

Mohandas Gandhi.

Listening

Take some time to breathe deeply and to calm yourself. Bring yourself back to your identification with the resentful one. Listen and acknowledge that you try to be dutiful. Invite your heart to speak to you about your feeling inadequate before others. Listen and identify who you've given the power to upset you and hold you hostage in angry feelings. Stay, listen, and give time to hear all that your heart wants to say.

Try to see if there isn't also a cry in your heart to believe "I am a sister. I am a brother. I'm not better or worse than anyone else." Hear that cry as a true call to claim yourself as a full member of the human family. Listen to your true heart telling you that you are a precious and cherished person, among so many other wonderful people, who search and struggle like you, and who one day will die, like you. Listen and try to plumb the depths of your truth.

Journaling

Try to put into words the inner dialogue that took place during your listening time. Perhaps zero in on some of the people or events that destroyed your image of yourself as enough. Give yourself freedom to express the burden that you carry.

Move slowly to write your insights into the truth about you and about your amazing life. In this sacred space, question how you can reclaim the truth and move away from feeling inadequate. Write your gratitude for those beautiful gifts that have been showered upon you in the course of your years. Finally, express your desire to stand fully in the true beauty of who you are.

Communing

Abide with the Presence of the Sacred with you in this time and place. Speak of all you have heard and written. Ask to be mindful of the words of Jesus, "My Father and I will come to you and we will

*You who live in the shelter of the Most High
and who abide in the shadow of the Almighty,
will say to the Lord, "Oh Lord, you are my
refuge in whom I trust. . . . You will conceal me
with your pinions and under your wings I will
find safety. . . . I shall not fear the terror of the
night nor the arrow that flies by day, nor the
plague that stalks in the darkness, nor the
scourge that wastes at noon. A thousand may
fall at my side, ten thousand fall at my right,
but all this will never approach me. . . . Because I have made the Most High my dwelling
place, no evil shall befall me. . . . For God will
command the angels concerning me, to guard
me in all my ways. On their hands they will
bear me up. . . . "Those who love me, I will
deliver," says the Lord. "I will protect those who
know my name. When they call to me, I will
answer them; I will be with them in trouble. I
will rescue them and honor them. With long
life I will satisfy them, and show them my
salvation."*

Psalm 91, paraphrased.

make a home in you." Ask to be empowered to believe, to feel at home with Love present, and to live from that sacred place. Speak your heart and listen for the response.

Heart speaks to heart.

A Wisdom Practice for Those on a Spiritual Journey

Practice #5 BEFRIEND THE POOR

In the parable there were two very different perspectives about the young runaway. The elder child was scandalized and broke relational ties with a younger brother. But the brokenhearted father never lost hope for the return of a beloved child. The former maintained his illusions of a perfect world and refused permission to his sibling to experiment or to fail. The latter with more life experience accepted the mystery of human suffering with compassion and tenderness.

At L'Arche Daybreak I initially felt exhilarated in an environment acceptable for people with disabilities to *not* have their lives totally together! But not long afterward my own life fell apart and I was the one who was suddenly and totally unable to function! Heartfelt prayers with gestures of love were heaped upon me from some of the weakest members of the community, a few of whom gently put a hand on my shoulder and said, "Don't worry, Henri. You're going to be OK." With the outpouring of this genuine tenderness in my weakest hour, I began to penetrate Jesus' words, "Blessed are the poor."

As a spiritual practice consider fostering a real relationship with one who is visibly marginalized. Look beyond bizarre behavior, unfamiliar humor, or a broken body and offer mutual friendship. Step beyond fear, beyond being a do-gooder, beyond controlling the relationship, and discover beyond the handicap a precious sister or brother. From your unlikely friend you may be surprised to feel that you, too, are truly lovable and blessed just as you are.

6

homecoming to gratitude

The first rule is simply this:
Live this life and do whatever is done, in a
spirit of thanksgiving.
Abandon attempts to achieve security, they are
futile,
give up the search for wealth, it is demeaning,
quit the search for salvation, it is selfish,
and come to comfortable rest in the certainty
that those who participate in this life
with an attitude of thanksgiving will receive its
full promise.

From *Always We Begin Again: The Benedictine Way of Living* by John McQuiston II, 1996, Morehouse Publishing, Harrisburg, PA, pp. 17–18.

Moving away from resentment requires moving toward something more positive, and that something is thankfulness. Why? Because gratitude is the opposite of resentment and gratuity moves us away from the world of earning-and-repayment in love.

Listen to what Jesus says to Peter: "When you were young, you girded yourself and went where you wanted to go. When you grow old, you will stretch out your hand and someone else will gird you and lead you where you rather would not go." Jesus' way is the opposite of psychological teaching. That way of the world proposes that in our youth we are dependent and others tell us what to do, while as older adults we can go our own way, be independent, and do what we want.

Jesus, however, invites us to a *new* way, the opposite of this shallow way of living. He is saying, "When you were young in the spiritual life you were in control and made your choices about what you believed or did not believe. But when you grow older and more mature spiritually, you are to allow those around you to gird you and lead you where you rather would not go! Jesus' path leads toward an intimacy with the Divine that supports the growth of faithful, unconditional love in our primary relationships, as well as growth in respectful care for those beyond our inner circles with whom we are interrelated in the human family. "Love your enemies" is tough love and it is the path of our return from the corrosion of resentment to the joy of gratitude. Relinquishing the need to control and dominate family members, colleagues, and friends is "the way, the truth, and the life" that Jesus speaks about. Jesus lovingly challenges us, saying, "Give up shaping and controlling events and people, and be willing to be girded and led."

Jesus' invitation is a call to abandon relational safety zones and become vulnerable, interdependent, and obedient to the voice of unconditional love. It implies living gratefully and finding an intimate solidarity with brothers and sisters in the human family. This identification with people so different from ourselves is really wonderful but also extremely difficult, because instead of claiming control in these relationships we open ourselves to an unknown future with many surprises. Solidarity with others requires attitude changes, acceptance of difference, and the struggle to live humbly and respectfully with them. It urges us to put aside self-righteousness and become equal in our relationships.

Who, then, girds us and leads us to be transformed into loving human beings? Our loved ones, spouses, partners, and children, as well as our leaders and those marginalized by society who are also the instruments of our transformation—all lead us in certain aspects of our lives. Each one wraps us in the swaddling bands of commitment before taking us far beyond our expectations of love to the path of greater and great intimacy and gratitude. Married life is wonderful but it is also a furnace of transformation. Family demands fidelity that hurts, friendships test our ability to love beyond our feelings, world events call us to more compassion than we think we have, and death is an invitation to hope beyond what we see

Adam was one of my housemates. . . . He was the first person I was asked to care for when I joined the L'Arche Daybreak community in Toronto where he lived. . . . Adam was my friend, my teacher, and my guide: an unusual friend, because he couldn't express affection and love in the way most people do; an unusual teacher, because he couldn't think reflectively or articulate ideas or concepts; an unusual guide, because he couldn't give me any concrete direction or advice. . . . Adam's death touched me deeply because for me he was the one who more than any book or professor led me to the person of Jesus.

From *Adam: God's Beloved* by Henri J. M. Nouwen, 1997, Orbis Books, Maryknoll, NY, pp. 15–16.

and feel. Jesus came among us and lived the way of gratitude through his communion with the one he called "Father." He entered into his passion, lost control of his life, and walked the narrow path of return while forgiving his enemies.

He told his disciples, "To you I open the Psalms and Prophets in Scriptures so that you will understand that I had to struggle and suffer and then later enter into glory." Jesus' whole life is a life that moves from action, control, preaching, teaching, and performing miracles to passion where everything is done to him. He's arrested, flogged, spit upon, crowned, and nailed to the Cross, and he doesn't control any of it. The fulfillment of Jesus' whole life is not in what he did, but in what was done to him. Passion. Action is control. Passion is allowing ourselves to be emptied out at the hands of others, so that the glory of God can be revealed in us.

It is obvious that the turning away from resentment for those who, like me, identify with the elder son is probably much more difficult than returning from a life of dissipation displayed by the young prodigal, because resentment is much less overtly obvious than dissipation. Most often, the resentful person is not even aware of being lost in the first place.

Identifying with the elder son in the story revealed to me my profound sorrow and how I have spent a good deal of my life building a stone wall of protection around my heart. Now, when I actually *hear* the truth about my hardness of heart, it seemed as though one of the stones is being taken out of my protective wall. This wounds me and makes me frightened and then angry. It's a big struggle. I'm trying to become much more aware and less fearful. I'm consciously trying a

But if you do not clear a decent shelter for your sorrow, and instead reserve most of the space inside you for hatred and thoughts of revenge—from which new sorrows will be born for others—then sorrow will never cease in this world and will multiply. And if you have given sorrow the space its gentle origins demand, then you may truly say: life is beautiful and so rich. So beautiful and so rich that it makes you want to believe in God.

From *An Interrupted Life, and Letters from Westerbork* by Etty Hillesum, 1996, Henry Holt and Company, New York, p. 97.

different response: "Don't be afraid. Let the stones be taken away and be grateful. Go beyond your comfort zone and trust. Have courage and open yourself to your heart's deeper desire, and let the wall fall down."

Far from making me feel safe, this practice frightens me. But at the same time space is opening up within me like a hollow cave that allows me to receive other people with acceptance and wonder. My faltering efforts to be grateful for my loved ones in family and community give me energy and a real joy. I tend to sense the voice of Love Divine whispering in my heart, "Be thankful and find more room for joy in your life. Recognize everything in your life as a gift and consciously give thanks. Open yourself and allow me to remove your heart of stone and give you a heart of flesh."

I'm having to name my fear of the implications of being equal with others. I'm having to acknowledge my attitude of superiority and self-righteousness. I'm coming face-to-face with my anger, my unresolved conflicts, my unwillingness to engage emotionally, and my lack of forgiveness of those I am committed to love. I'm so

aware that my return is
impossible without God's
help, because it is so hard
for me not to act from my
angry feelings, my jealousy,
and my enormous fear of
losing myself if I become
one with others. To live

*Overcome any bitterness because you were not
up to the magnitude of the pain entrusted to
you. Like the mother of the world you are carrying the pain of the world in your heart.*

A Sufi saying.

gratefully I need to talk about my difficulties and become more ac-
countable to my mentor. I need solitude to reflect on my relationships, and I need time to ask God to help me by giving me the love
I lack.

Finally, let me give one more scriptural example. Perhaps you are
familiar with the parable of the eleventh hour, paraphrased below.
The full text may be found in Matthew 20:1–16.

The owner of the vineyard goes out early in the morning and
asks people to work the day for him for a just wage.

They come, and then he similarly recruits new people three
or four more times as the day progresses, promising a just pay-
ment for work done.

At the end of the day the owner of the vineyard gives each
worker the same wage, beginning with those he hired last.

Honestly, this treatment of the workers by the master is very hard
to accept. I think it is terribly unfair. The people who came and

I am still running, running from that
*   knowledge,*
that eye, that love from which there is no
*   refuge.*
For you meant only love, and love,
and I felt only fear, and pain.

From *Teaching a Stone to Talk* by Annie Dillard,
1982, Harper and Row, New York, p. 141.

worked only for the last hour get as much money as those who worked the whole day in the vineyard.

On reflection, though, the workers' and our reaction to this behavior is very interesting indeed! We feel angry and we rationalize by our "justice" mentality. At least the landowner could have paid the early-comers first and sent them away so that they wouldn't see what the latecomers got! But no! Right in the face of those early-comers who worked the whole day the master pays a day's wage to the latecomers. It follows that those watching are expecting to receive more, but they don't get it! That's offensive. It not only insults all *their* feelings of justice but ours as well!

Do not judge, and you will not be judged; be-
cause the judgements you give are the judge-
ments you will get. . . . Why do you observe the
splinter in your brother's eye and never notice
the great log in your own? . . . Hypocrite! Take
the log out of your own eye first, and then you
will see clearly enough to take the splinter out
of your brother's eye.

From the Jerusalem Bible, Matthew 7:1–5.

Our reaction is so interesting. This same parable was adapted for a group of children and went like this:

There was a father who

had many children and he went to the oldest and said, "I want you to help me out today."

The child worked hard for the father the whole day. Later the father called the second child, who was younger, and later still a third.

By mid afternoon all the children were engaged in the task with the exception of the two-year-old baby. At the end of the day, the father called all the children together and began by giving the little two-year-old the same reward that he gave to each other child.

In the group of children to whom the story was told, *nobody* thought the father was unfair. They responded, "Wasn't it fun that the toddler got the same as everyone else?" Isn't it something to think about that; children enjoyed that everyone got the same from the funny father who was so good with the kids! Indeed, I had never even considered working in the vineyard as an enormous privilege. To work for my dad the whole day together with my brothers and sisters . . . isn't that wonderful? And isn't it great that those who came only at the last minute and couldn't work the whole day received so much?

This makes me realize how self-righteous I am and what a weird way of thinking I have adopted because I resent the late-comers receiving the same as me. I wonder why I forget how great a privilege it is to spend the day with

O, that I might walk in the Light with a grate-
     ful heart,
And radiate peace to the world.

From *Psalms for Praying* by Nan C. Merrill, 1996, The Continuum International Publishing Group, New York, Psalm 101, p. 207.

brothers and sisters doing what I was asked to do by the one who loves me most. What prevents me from rejoicing in my father's generosity with those I love the most?

So, too, when the father of the prodigal son calls for a party he's far from considering that his eldest child will feel excluded. Rather he is saying, "Come in, one and all, because your brother has returned! Be grateful with me for his return! See my goodness toward the one in the family who hasn't made it easy for me. Note that I celebrate my child's return. Come, join the party, and learn to be grateful like me!"

This movement to be grateful rather than judgmental of others is a real turning and a profound conversion. The wonderful side of it is that we discover not only how much we need the unconditional Lover to give us love but also how deeply we are connected with others as brothers and sisters. This passage from resentment to gratitude confirms us in our humanity.

And in the passage of return there is a further step to be taken. The return is not just about you and me, but it has to do with our response to another person's resentment. Seeing what we do, and working to change, there is an urge to critically judge resentment seen in others. This is important because we each must choose our reactions to the anger and pain of others. It is when we are primarily giving thanks for our lives that we have the potential to receive another's anger and judgment while remaining upright and letting it move through us. When we are looking for occasions to be grateful we hear anger and pain in a new way and can more readily accept it as being theirs and not ours. It is in that spirit that we try simply to receive it without

judgment. This is only possible as we adopt thanks-
giving as our way of living.
Otherwise *their* resentment
connects with *ours* and that
only makes things worse.
In the grateful life we no
longer listen to another's

To understand the enemy both within us and outside of us is an important part of forgiveness.

From *Becoming Human* by Jean Vanier, 1998, House of Anansi Press, Toronto, p. 162.

resentment as an affirmation of our own. Nor do we judge. We simply receive it in love.

To be able to lovingly receive the dark judgments of another is a painfully slow process with many ups and downs and much learning. There is a fine line between accepting another's anger and accepting abuse, and each of us must know the difference and not accept abusive treatment. You and I do not have to agree with another's ways, nor do we have to pretend that that person's treatment of us was not wrong. But it is important to objectively acknowledge the other's unique story and especially the suffering of the one who offends us. When I feel hurt I must try to stand up for myself and at the same time try not to project judgment. I must work to accept how the other person's individual story is a whole world of joy and pain just like mine. I know this is the way for a growing solidarity between us.

Ever so gradually I'm learning to offer my neighbor permission to be different from me and to make unique choices that are different from the ones that I would make. My awareness of how each one has an irreplaceable position in the human family is opening

Dear Lord, having been plunged into this solitude and with my hands outstretched, I become more accustomed to the darkness. More alone than I could ever be, I'm learning to live the death that you have chosen for me. It is more painful than any other death but my eyes are adapting in the darkness. I begin to distinguish the disguises of your love, deeper than any love I've ever known. And slowly it dawns on me that my loneliness is turning me towards you. The death is very deep, but within it is also joyous life. In this darkest darkness I am finally aware of light, your light. I begin to see where "home" is for me. Love is being born in me over and over again. Thank you, Lord. Thank you.

From the tapes of Henri Nouwen's workshop.

me to allow space for the beauty of the differences that exist between us. It's my firm conviction that returning from resentment to gratitude offers me a sense of deep belonging in our vast and precious human family as well as with the One who created us in all our beauty and diversity.

Listening

Find space and time for stillness within and around you. Wait. Without going back to read, simply listen for the images or insights that struck you while reading this chapter. What are these passages saying to you about your present life? Listen and allow your heart time to express its yearning for wholeness, for integrity, and for transparency. Try not to fear the silence and wait with stillness for your heart to articulate the deep stirrings within. Listen for your heart cry to come home to yourself.

Journaling

Begin by writing something wonderful that happened to you in your life. Perhaps it was an experience with one of your parents, or when you fell in love, or meeting someone who impacted your life journey. What else happened that was important for you? Continue to write about the valued meetings, the important insights, the unexpected "miracles," and the surprises that brought you joy.

Write in a spirit of gratitude for people and moments of import. Write about good things in your life that you take for granted—including life itself! Let your pen describe your treasured history.

If there be anywhere on earth a lover of God is always safe, I know nothing of it, for it was not shown to me. But this was shown: that in falling and rising again we are always kept in the same precious love.

Julian of Norwich.

Communing

Remember you are surrounded by the presence of the divine Breath who communicates with you in the deep recesses of your heart. Enter and speak into that presence the honest gratitude for all the good things you have received. Try to go beyond your hesitations with belief and unbelief, beyond the ambiguities of your life, and entrust all to the One who knows and loves you most completely. Allow yourself to give thanks with joy.

Heart speaks to heart.

A Wisdom Practice for Those on a Spiritual Journey

Practice #6   CLAIM HOME ON THE WAY HOME

In reality or in spirit, each of the young adults in the parable left in disillusionment but was later received home. Conforming or not, polite or not, contrite or not, each sibling belonged in the family and each was entitled to unique love without condition. Jesus points toward such a home for us when he says, "I am going to prepare a place for you."

Meanwhile, however hard I try, I do not find a *permanent* home of safety, acceptance, and creative caring. Only occasionally in the smile, the kind word, the embrace, or the gift of friendship do I have a fleeting taste of "home on the way home." But my months in solitude made me grateful for such unique gifts of caring. They reminded me of another, greater Love. Now I feel called to receive any momentary affirmation simply and with gratitude. Further, I'm challenged to freely confirm others by saying in so many words, "I'm so glad *you* are here and we are together."

Jesus teaches us "Love your neighbor as yourself." If we are too preoccupied and too busy, we fail to connect in simple exchanges of love with others. Love doesn't need long speeches. Rather, love is attentive to fleeting moments of peace, kindness, friendship, and compassion. Love invites us as a spiritual discipline to communicate with our loved ones more and more from hearts broken open by compassion.

part three

Home Is Receiving Love and Giving Love

7

the primal relationship

Jesus' life is an invitation for us to believe, not primarily in him but in the *relationship* between himself and the God whom he

But look, I am going to seduce her and lead her into the desert and speak to her heart.

From the Jerusalem Bible, Hosea 2:16.

names "Father." Furthermore, Jesus comes into the world to communicate to those of us who are listening that this very same *relationship* is uniquely available to each one of us. By his life and death Jesus announces the yearning in the heart of Love Divine, to be in relationship with each individual person. For you or I to engage this primal encounter is for us to return "home."

This *relationship* between Jesus and the One who sent him into the world is *the* central focus of Jesus' whole life and teaching. He urges us to see how he comes to us not on his own but sent and in *relationship* with God the Creator-Spirit. Jesus' whole mission, his life, words, works, disgrace, and glory, are only relevant because of his *relationship* with the One who sent him. Everything about his life is forever in *relationship* with the One he calls Father. He is passionate when he says, "Believe in me," which means "Believe that I am sent by the One who calls me Beloved." It means "Believe every word I speak, because I heard these words in *relationship* with my Father." "Believe in me" means "Believe that every work I do is not mine alone but is also my Spirit-Father-God working through me." It means "Believe that the glory I receive does not belong to me but is given to me by the One with whom I am intimately united in my spirit."

Hold tightly to the hand of faith

For strength through deep valleys

Learn to trust in the One,

Who is ever your companion and guide.

From *Psalms for Praying* by Nan C. Merrill, 1996, The Continuum International Publishing Group, New York, Psalm 119, p. 264.

This is a union so total and so full that there is not even the slightest place for an experience of absence or separation. To be *in* that relationship is to be home in the deepest possible sense of the word.

This is new for me, that my following of Jesus calls me to believe not only in the full communion between Jesus and the One who sent him into the world but to believe in *my* communion with the One who sent *me* into the world. Jesus says, "Philip, how can you say 'Show us the Father'? Don't you know that when you see me, you see the Father also?" Jesus is one who is never alone, but always bonded in love without the slightest distance, the slightest fear, or the slightest hesitation between himself and the One who sent him into the world.

Jesus the man mirrors an "enfleshed" relationship with Unconditional Love to reveal how to "be home" in our humanity. "Who sees me, sees the Father. Who believes in me, believes in the Father. I and the Father are one. I am in the Father and the Father is in me." At his baptism, Jesus and others heard the voice of Love Divine: "You are my beloved son. My favor rests on you." Later Jesus says, "As the Father has loved me, so I also love you. The Father and I are one." The words "My favor rests on you" are said to us. The relationship is available to us and to see Jesus is to know the relationship.

Jesus never, never, never makes a distinction between his relationship with Unconditional Love and ours. Jesus never says, "I know the great Spirit fully and you can know a little bit about the Holy One." He doesn't say, "I can do great things in the name of God-Mother, and you can maybe do a few things." No. Jesus instead tells us, "All the things I've heard because of my communion with the Indwelling Beloved I tell you because I want you to have the same experience of knowing Love that I have. All the things I do in the name of the One who loves me so much, you have power to do, too. In fact, you will accomplish even greater things than me. And all

I call you friends, because I have made known to you everything I have learned from my Father.

From the Jerusalem Bible, John 15:15.

the glory I receive from the One who affirms me in my humanity is available for you to receive as well. You are to be as fully the adult child of Unconditional Love as me. You are to live a communion with Love itself that is so intimate that you also become the visibility of Love's Spirit present in the world."

I really need to hear this, and I believe that you do, too. Jesus came not simply to tell us about a loving Creator who is far away and who, from there, cares for us. Not at all! Jesus came to offer us the same full communion with the Spirit-Father-Mother-Lover that he enjoys, where he is in no way smaller than the One who sent him.

The word for that intimate communion between Jesus and God is "Spirit." It captures an affiliation that is so total, so loaded, so holy, so sacred, so complete that it lacks absolutely nothing. The Greek word for "spirit" is *pneuma*, which means "breath." The bond between Jesus and the One he calls Father is like breathing. Breathing is so central and intimate that we aren't even aware that we're breathing. If we become aware of it, it's because something is wrong. Otherwise we are simply breath-

Dear Child of God, all of us are meant to be contemplatives. Frequently we assume that this is reserved for some rare monastic life, lived by special people who alone have been called by God. But the truth of the matter is that each one of us is meant to have that space inside where we can hear God's voice. God is available to all of us. God says, "Be still and know that I am God."

From *God Has a Dream: A Vision of Hope for Our Times* by Desmond Tutu, 2004, Doubleday, New York, p. 101.

ing and no one comments on it by saying, "Oh my, you're breathing!" or "I notice you're breathing really nicely today!" No. We don't ever talk about it. It is just part of our lives and we just breathe and our breath is life.

The relationship between Jesus and the Father, like our breathing, is immediate, urgent, and near. Jesus tells us after his resurrection, "It's good for you that I'm going, because if I go, I will then send you my breath, my Spirit. Then you will fully live in me as I live in you."

The parable of the prodigal son invites our reflection on this great, great revelation of amazing good news. The story embodies the *relationship*. Look again at the Rembrandt painting of a father laying hands on his young son. Feel those hands and remember how such loving tenderness affects us and makes us live. We may know the anguish of not being touched with love, but these incredible hands lift us from our knees in total forgiveness while healing our broken hearts.

The eyes, the hands, and the cape image the profound blessedness, lasting love, and "home" to which we can return again and again. Claim the words celebrating *your* return: "Quick! You are to have the best robe; here is a ring for your finger and sandals for your feet." Saint Paul tells us, "You will receive a new garment of the children of God and you will be like God." That is the best robe. The ring is the ring of the inheritor, the ring that is given to the inheritors of the kingdom. And the sandals ensure that we walk in safety. Lastly, "The calf we have been fattening will be killed in your honor; we will celebrate by having a fiesta." The banquet is a celebration of heaven where our differences bless us as family, and where we feast together from the same table.

Jesus "did not cling to his equality with God, but emptied himself," for an experience of total communion. He uses these images for a *relationship* that is, in fact, much, much more than the human images of daughter, son, mother, or father. What is so compelling is that we become like the one we love. Our return "home" is to relate intimately in spirit with Love and also to *become* Love for others: compassionate, forgiving, creative, spirit-filled lovers in the best sense of the word.

Listening

Breathe deeply and find a still rhythm for exhaling preoccupations and for inhaling peace. In your imagination take your place silently beside Jesus and walk together up the mountain in the evening. Sit apart and watch him situate himself to pray. Watch him enter into communion with the One who sent him into the world. Imagine his communion with Love Divine. Stay and listen.

Now go alone to the mountaintop and imagine yourself in the presence of the One who sent you into the world. Be still. Wait. Don't speak but rest in the presence. Listen.

The desert fathers counselled, "Go into your cell, and your cell will teach you everything." Set aside a period of time in nature or at home, at a church or temple, a library or anywhere you will not be disturbed. Sit, walk, meditate, pray, read, whatever pleases you. Pay attention.

From *Sabbath: Restoring the Sacred Rhythm of Rest* by Wayne Muller, 1999, Bantam Books, New York, p. 178.

Journaling

Write what you witnessed on the mountaintop. Note your feelings while you were present there with Jesus in communion with Love Unending. What was difficult for you? Write what you heard in your imagination. What were you feeling as you ascended the mountain alone? Write what transpired as you tried to imagine yourself in communion with God's Spirit. Write your emotions, what you heard, your thoughts, and your feelings.

Communing

Quietly enter into that privileged place in the depths of your heart and abide with Love. Give yourself permission to rest there with or without words. Commune.

Heart speaks to heart.

A Wisdom Practice for Those on a Spiritual Journey

Practice #7   CLAIM YOUR INNER "SPIRIT" LIFE

In the parable both siblings are preoccupied with themselves because neither has inwardly matured enough to feel responsible for belonging in this, their family of origin. The mature one, the father figure, lives with a deep interiority and is fully composed, fully accepting of his position in the family, and uniquely committed to each family member.

Unfortunately my interiority up to now has been to claim my many disturbing "spirits"; angry feelings, painful dreams, troubling fantasies, and hurts around unresolved relationships, more than to be attentive to the Spirit of Jesus, who also occupies my inner landscape. Now I'm working to adopt the practice of speaking directly and often to the God-Spirit living within me.

Jesus announced the availability of the Giver of Life for an inner relationship of communion with each one of us. He said,

> "If you love me you will keep my word, and my Father will love you and we shall come to you and make a home in you." (John 14:23)
>
> "I shall ask the Father, who will give you another Paraclete to be with you for ever, the Spirit of Truth whom the world can never accept since it neither sees nor knows God; but you know the Spirit with you and in you." (John 14:16–17)

In the Scripture Jesus is very often found to be in communion with the Divine Love. He goes to the mountain and spends the whole night in prayer to God. He speaks his inner union aloud on the Cross: "Father, forgive them, for they know not what they do."

touch and blessing

We always want someone else to change so that we will feel good. But has it ever struck you that even if your wife changes or your husband changes, what does that do to you? You're just as vulnerable as before; you're just as idiotic as before; you're just as asleep as before. You are the one who needs to change, who needs to take medicine. You keep insisting, "I feel good because the world is right." Wrong! "The world is right because I feel good." That's what all the mystics are saying.

Anthony de Mello.

There was a time in my life when I became focused on how my parents had wounded me and I remember wishing that they had behaved differently. Listening to others, however, I saw how they too experienced times of feeling primarily hurt by parents, partners, relatives, friends, or those in their church community. Isn't it true that we have been

hurt because parents and others were unable to reflect unconditional love to us? Perhaps they held on to us too tightly or seemed to
push us away. They wounded us not because they wanted to wound
us, but because they also were people who were loved imperfectly
by others. Each one of us, as well as all who went before us, share
the human condition and suffer from being loved imperfectly. We
are not meant to stop at simply feeling the pain of these wounds,
nor are we to become stuck in guilt or accusations. Rather this
whole experience is to move us toward accepting a relationship
with God's living Spirit of Unconditional Love. Our spiritual journey is nothing more than a return to the intimacy, the safety, and
the acceptance of that very first relationship with Love, that is
uniquely present and at home within each one of us.

I am aware that I have been deeply loved and enabled in my life.
I move and speak to you, I relate with many people, I walk and
smile because I've been loved so immensely. I owe a debt of gratitude to many, many people for loving me into this, my existence,
despite knowing that those very same people who loved me were
also wounded and broken people like me. I acknowledge that I am
sometimes surprised to still feel pain because of those old hurts,
and when I do, I have a hard time claiming the immense love that
I've been given. When I live from the pain I doubt myself and have
trouble in relationships. My difficulty is that when I feel the hurts I
go looking for love externally from other wounded people instead
of claiming and communing with the One who knows me, loves me
as I am, and makes a home in my heart.

Jesus taught us about the whole movement of God's love with

We who lived in concentration camps can re-member the men who walked through the huts comforting others, giving away their last piece of bread. They may have been few in number . . . but they offer sufficient proof that everything can be taken from a man but one thing: the last of his freedoms—to choose one's attitude in any given set of circumstances, to choose one's own way.

From *Man's Search for Meaning* by Viktor E. Frankl, 1963, Washington Square Press, New York, p. 104.

bread. His actions with bread in Scripture image his and our lives as beloved children of God. In the multiplication of the loaves at the Last Supper, Jesus took the bread first. Bread was chosen as God chooses each one of us uniquely as a beloved daughter or son. After the bread was in his hands Jesus blessed it, just as our Creator confirms each of us as beloved children. The bread is broken as Jesus was broken on the Cross and as we are broken because of undeserved suffering in our lives. Finally, the bread was given for the life of others, just as Jesus' life was given, and ours is to be given. Jesus does this many, many times: taking, blessing, breaking, and giving. We experience the joys of being chosen and blessed. And we are broken not because we are cursed but because, like Jesus, passion moves us to *com*passion and to be given for others who suffer.

The first biblical story about the garden in Eden describes how God walked with Adam and Eve in a relationship of unconditional love. When they doubted and turned away from God's word toward each other's word, they experienced nakedness, anxiety, and fear. Adam responds to God's "Where are you?" in the garden with "I was afraid because I was naked, so I hid." Original sin names this failure to trust the original relationship. Original sin is following the temptation to experience the first love from other people and things. Fortunately Adam and Eve's pain and anxiety touched the very heart of God, who sent Jesus into the world to personally witness to the first-love relationship.

Working occasionally with prisoners in the past, I was humbled to realize how those deeply wounded individuals became criminals because of their desperate need to be noticed, respected, heard, or free from their sense of total alienation. Most of them were frantic to feel loved. Being rejected plunged them into terror and to believing it is better to kill than to be killed.

With pain and gratitude O Divine Spirit, I
come to you
with all my brothers and sisters on the planet,
I pause with them to receive your love.
Help each one of us to know truth, and to more
fully claim our individual belovedness.
May your Spirit be in each one to accomplish
new miracles.

Adapted from Henri Nouwen's original manuscript of his workshop.

I truly feel that many acts of killing are not primarily because people are evil but because they are desperate. So often I have found so-called "felons" to be hungry for the safety of committed relationships with love and care. I saw how easily they cried and I heard them say, "What have I done? I only wanted to be recognized as someone of value. I longed to be part of a family with my wife and my children." Many of these brothers and sisters have never known or felt the safe touch of a loving hand.

Perhaps you and I need to look at suffering people in our world

Soul of Christ sanctify me

Body of Christ save me

Blood of Christ inebriate me

Water from the side of Christ wash me

Passion of Christ strengthen me

O good Jesus hear me

In your wounds hide me

Suffer me not to be separated from thee

From the malicious foe defend me

In the hour of my death call me

And bid me come to thee

That with the saints I may praise thee

Forever and ever. Amen

Prayer of Saint Ignatius, quoted by Henri Nouwen in
original tapes of his workshop.

from a new perspective. We all know the lonely person in others or ourselves who, through so many disturbing behaviors, is asking, "Please recognize me, please love me." Human suffering is so often an expression of our extreme need to feel genuinely loved, and when we know nothing about the first love, we turn to others who cannot offer us the love we need. It is then that the cry moves us toward violence. "I can't do without you. You must stay with me." Suddenly instead of caressing we grab and that frightens the other person away. It's daunting to see how the grabbing, the slapping, the biting, the violence, and sometimes the rape are really the other side of our desperate need to love and be loved.

Rembrandt was able to paint the prodigal's return only after a long life of immense suffering. Few people have cried as many tears as Rembrandt, for his children who died and for his wives who died. His tears and suffering opened his eyes to understand the love of a God who wept so much for a lost child as to become almost blind, but with a blindness that reveals inner light. Rembrandt understood and could paint the one whose love does not prevent his child leaving for a foreign land where he will suffer. Rembrandt used a human image to illustrate how the One who relates intimately with us offers us freedom, is conscious of our suffering as a beloved child, and watches for our return.

For wisdom is quicker to move than any
*   motion;*
she is so pure, she pervades and permeates all
*   things,*
She is a breath of the power of God,
pure emanation of the glory of the Almighty;
so nothing impure can find its way into her.
For she is a reflection of the eternal light,
untarnished mirror of God's active power,
and image of his goodness.

From the Jerusalem Bible, Wisdom 7:24–26.

Nothing, neither tears nor near blindness, prevents the recognition of the favored one returning home.

Look at the hands of the father in the painting. Very few people notice at first glance that there are two different hands, one of a man and the other of a woman. Rembrandt knew that the Divine was not merely a man looking upon creation from the sky, and he understood something about the Creator that Jesus wanted us to know. He experienced the God of Jesus as One with all the best characteristics of mothers and fathers and more. Rembrandt painted the hand of the woman from an earlier painting of the Jewish bride. She has very delicate, gentle, and tender hands that speak about who she is as woman—protecting, caring, and inordinately in love. The hand of the man is Rembrandt's own hand. It speaks of who he is as father, supporter, defender, and giver of freedom. After a long life and having lived the death of both of his wives and all of his children, Rembrandt understood the depths of holding and letting go, of offering protection and freedom, of maternity and paternity. That's how he was able to paint this image of God toward the end of his life. His suffering had somehow not made him bitter or resentful but had rather opened him to recognize Love's yearning heart for intimate, unique relationships with daughters and sons. Rembrandt was able to paint the Giver of Life as a most compassionate and loving Counselor, holding, blessing, letting go, and receiving back into safety the immature but emerging adult children of creation. Look at the cape. It is like a Gothic arch, very protecting. It is like the wings of a mother bird surrounding her children. "In the shadow of your wings I take refuge till the storms of destruction pass by" (Psalms 57:1). The touch of blessing on the shoulders of the adult child is the touch of maternity and paternity in its perfection.

Once I heard Jean Vanier, founder of the communities of L'Arche around the world, speak about hands. He described the hands that gently encircle a wounded bird as being hands that are also open to allow movement and freedom to fly. Jean believes that each of us needs to have both these hands around us. One says, "I've got you and I hold you safe because I love you and I'll never be apart from you. Don't be afraid." The other says, "Go, my child, find your way, make mistakes, learn, suffer, grow, and become who you need to be. Don't be afraid. You are free and I am always near." Jean Vanier imagines these two hands as the hands of Unconditional Love.

The word blessing in Latin is *benedicture*. *Bene* means "good," and *dicture* means "to say." *Benedicere,* and likewise, "blessing," means "to announce good things and to confirm one another." In the picture, the touch of hands is the blessing of the one who passionately affirms and loves the child that he and his wife brought into the world. If he is listening at all, this young prodigal can only hear "I'm so thankful you are home. I've watched you grow and I've always wanted you close to me as an adult. I've missed you terribly and I've been waiting for you. You are my cherished one, beloved of my heart." This blessing must have pierced the heart of the young adolescent.

Jesus' whole mission was to witness to our participation in this blessed relationship with the One who breathes love without conditions. When he told the parable of the prodigal son he was aware of how this sacred, sacred event of parent blessing the child was engraved in the history of God's people. Abraham blessed Isaac, and later Isaac blessed Jacob. In giving us this story Jesus wanted each of us to see, to understand, and to believe that loving hands of blessing are forever resting upon us. The Creator of the galaxies lives, whispers uniquely good things about us in our hearts, and urges us to rise up and use our freedom to become compassionate peacemakers in our world. This bond of love that touches each one of our lives from the very beginning of our creation to the very end of time and beyond is our original blessing.

When you and I are home in this relationship, we find ourselves in the heart of the One that Jesus addresses as Father. We reside in the intimacy of the womb of Love Itself. Looking out from the heart of

How glorious is your dwelling place
  O Loving Creator of the universe!
My soul longs, yes, aches for
  the abode of the Beloved;
All that is within me sings for joy
  to the living Heart of Love!
Even as the sparrow finds a home,
  and the swallow a nesting place,
  where its young are raised within
    Your majestic creation,
You invite us to dwell within
  Your Heart.

From *Psalms for Praying* by Nan C. Merrill, 1996, The Continuum International Publishing Group, New York, Psalm 84, p. 174.

Love, our own hearts bleed with compassion, because from there we are seeing as God sees. From this intimate connection with God we grow to become like the One we love. You and I, along with all members of the human family, are blessed people with the blessing of unconditional love that will never be taken away. We are also people who offer compassion to those who suffer.

Jesus tells us that he is our way. We find the way when we follow him through the pages of Scripture. There we see how he was constantly communing and in relationship with the One who sent him into the world. When suffering was part of the way, Jesus chose not to ask "Why?" He chose not to blame those who hurt him. He stood in his agony, intimately connected with the One who loved him and also forgiving and caring for those who so cruelly tortured and killed him. This is the way, and by offering us this way, Jesus gives us new eyes to look into our experience of suffering and of life.

True homecoming is choosing the way of Jesus, where we acknowledge the good and painful in our lives and we ask for patience and courage to forgive all those who have wounded us on the journey. Their love was limited and conditional, but it set us in search of that unconditional, unlimited love. This way takes us on a path through the desert of suffering to our hidden wholeness and to our utter beauty in the eyes of the One we name God.

Listening

In your stillness, listen and respond to the question "Who is your God?" Listen deeply for what you believe are the characteristics of the very Source of your life. Listen to how your heart relates to your God. Next look again at the painting of the meaningful but limited image of the One Jesus calls God. Listen to the Heart of all hearts longing for intimacy and togetherness. Imagine the eyes of the father figure moving from the son to embrace you and to invite you to take the place of the adult child. When you are ready, put your head on Love's breast and allow the tender female hand to touch you in gratitude for your return. Feel the strong male hand caress you with joy and thoughts of celebration. Listen to words of tenderness, welcome, and unconditional love directed toward you.

Journaling

Write of your mixed emotions under this embrace of welcome.

Be content with what you have;
rejoice the way things are.
When you realize there is nothing lacking,
the whole world belongs to you.

From *Sabbath: Restoring the Sacred Rhythm of Rest*
by Wayne Muller, 1999, Bantam Books, New York, p.
82; quoted from Lao-Tzu with no reference.

Communing

In awe and reverence listen to the words of affirmation and welcome. Take the Beloved's hands in yours and get to your feet. Look into the eyes of love and speak. Commune in love.

Heart speaks to heart.

Practice #8   RECEIVE MERCY

Neither of the young men in the parable had lived long enough to know about giving or receiving mercy. However, after suffering separation in their own unique ways, they were each offered a unique return from isolation into the family fold. With no conditions, the love figure at "home" blesses each of the children with forgiveness, mercy, and unconditional welcome.

I enjoy being strong and able to support those who feel vulnerable. I'm also a generous giver, but in my ever-present "earning" mentality, I feel nervous to receive kindness from others in view of having to always repay. I have mixed emotions about being welcomed home when I know this has not been my first leaving and will probably not be my last. But my life and my suffering are opening me to receive care, kindness, and support, with gratitude, and to feel worthy of love.

Let us be aware of small gestures of love offered us by others that remind us of our unique beauty. Let us try to gratefully accept the smile, the tender word, the caring embrace, and the recognition that affirms our personhood. These are but reminders of the overwhelming reception awaiting our every return to communion with God's Spirit, and that mercy is always available and always confirming the truth of our belovedness.

9

unconditional love

Liberation of the human heart . . . opens us up and leads us to the discovery of our common humanity . . . a journey from loneliness to a love that transforms, a love that grows in and through belonging. . . . The discovery of our common humanity liberates us from self-centered compulsions and inner hurts; it is the discovery that ultimately finds its fulfilment in forgiveness and in loving those who are our enemies. It is the process of truly becoming human.

From *Becoming Human* by Jean Vanier, 1998, House of Anansi Press, Toronto, p. 5.

It is a fact that we live because of being touched by the love of parents and others that is only a reflection of an even greater love. And there is no question that our relationships with family and others contributed to our feelings of being lovable or not so lovable. Our sense of ourselves was enhanced by true love and diminished because the love from family was imperfect. It seems to me that it is the limited experience of unlimited love that awakens us to the deep inner cry for someone to love us unconditionally.

Personally I know I need healing in my relationships with family and especially with my father. I remember him once saying to me, "I know you see me as authoritarian, and that is true. I am. But my question is, why can't you let me be that way?" He laughed as he went on, saying, "You are a psychologist. You have Freud and others who help you understand authoritarian personalities, and here you have one right in your own family. I do not understand how you have always lived your friendships with freedom but you cannot allow me to be free in the way I live my relationships." I answered, "You're absolutely right. Why not?"

However, deep inside I still feel a need for him to be different, because I read into his behavior that he tries to manipulate me by instructing me on how to make coffee, ordering me to get a haircut, insulting me by saying I am not old enough to drive his car, and by insisting on having the last word in almost every conversation. We do not understand each other at many levels, and I, at fifty-seven years of age, feel injured by the way he relates to me. So I know that I have to make many more concessions, accept him more as he is, and try harder to relate lovingly with him.

Because of this struggle, I *know* there has to be more, a higher love that sets me free from my need to change my father. Perhaps I'm not completely there yet, but I do believe that from the perspective of being fully loved by God it's possible for me to let go of those things that distress me about my father so as to be able to laugh with him and to be more grateful for who he is. Knowing I am loved prior to my father loving me inspires me to see him as he is: simply a man with

As for the future, your task is not to foresee, but to enable it. It is not for us to stalk the vision, the vision is stalking us.

A Native American saying.

a good and loving heart, important and little, like everyone else. Yes, he's a bit of a character, but why can I not smile when he is telling me how to make the coffee? I have a good feeling about giving my father permission to be who he is without conditions, even though I'm not yet fully able to do so. After all, I, too, am just a little man with many foibles and a loving heart trying to find my way. Claiming God's first love helps me enormously to surrender my unrealistic expectations and to really be grateful for the father I have.

It is good for us to "be with" and to forgive family members, partners, and children without needing to shape them in a violent way. It is liberating to accept that they are different from us, that they think and act in their own ways, and that they make different choices than we might make. It is important to liberate them to make their own mistakes and to learn life's lessons at their own pace. And finally, instead of wishing they had lived according to our expectations, how blessed we'd be to be grateful even when they weren't able to love us perfectly, and how loving it would be to allow them to die in peace. Jesus gives us good advice: "Leave your father, leave your mother, leave your sister, and leave your brother." He knows that letting our parents and siblings go free is creating space in us not only to welcome God's unconditional love but also to gradually become a compassionate parent figure for others.

More and more I sense that the opposite of love is not hate but fear. Even though I don't feel that I hate anyone, I do know that I am afraid that people will not love me if I act freely in my relationship. I see more and more clearly how this fear moves me toward isolation and violence. Let me explain.

Not having fully claimed myself as a beloved child of God I carry real and imagined suffering around being unloved, abused, rejected, and unacceptable. This false sense of being not very good awakens feelings of loneliness, fear, and anguish. From there I move out, sometimes frantically, to find acceptance in others. I divide my world between those on my side and those who are against me. In self-protection I cling to the few who respond to me, and I fearfully begin to challenge those who befriend my friends in case they steal affection away from me. I do this not because I am hateful, but because I am afraid and I view people with suspicion and see them as dangerous. When I sense danger, I become preoccupied with survival and I begin to build real or imagined walls to protect my space. Then, of course, I begin to hoard things for emergencies and I withhold emotions, money, knowledge, material things, and love in case another will become stronger or more successful than me.

I hear the cry of suffering sisters and brothers: "Look. You have

> *The practice of the trapeze has acquainted me with many unholy ghosts that hide in the dark regions of the psyche. . . . I am afraid of failure. I am afraid of what others will think of me. I am afraid I will embarrass myself. I am afraid I will lose control. I am afraid I can't trust you. I am afraid I will be abandoned if I do not measure up to your expectations.*

From *Learning to Fly: Reflections on Fear, Trust, and the Joy of Letting Go* by Sam Keen, 1999, Broadway Books, New York, pp. 36–37.

Everything we have is on loan. Our homes, businesses, rivers, closest relationship, bodies, and experiences, everything we have is ours in trust, and must be returned at the end of our use of it. As trustees we have the highest and strictest requirements of fiduciary duty: to use nothing for our sole benefit; to manage prudently; and to return that which has been in our care in as good or better condition than it was when given into our custody.

From *Always We Begin Again: The Benedictine Way of Living* by John McQuiston II, 1996, Morehouse Publishing, Harrisburg, PA, p. 52.

all these friends, all this knowledge, and silos full of grain. You have more than you need and I have not enough. I want some of what you have. Why don't you share with me and let me have part of your wealth?" But now fear is the master and I reply, "It's true that there's more than enough now, but you never know about tomorrow, so I cannot share with you."

When panic dominates my horizons I always anticipate the worst. Behind my walls I'm fearful people out there are plotting to tear them down, so I top them off with shards of broken glass and explosives. I've become violent toward unseen enemies. And I have also to worry that my explosives could topple my way instead of toward the enemy. Fear consumes me and prevents me following my inner aspirations to love and be loved.

I hope you can see that hatred is really secondary to the fear that consumes our inner space and compels us to build prisons around ourselves. I hope you can reflect how fear

Breeds feelings of being unsafe, unloved, and alone.
Makes us believe we won't be loved if we act freely.

Prompts us to divide the world between friends and
   enemies.

Inspires us to hoard.

Robs us of our capacity to love and be loved in return.

Obliges us to cling to people and things.

Limits our ability to relate with the Spirit of Love
   within.

When we freely allow fear to dominate and change us, we live in misery far from our home of unconditional love.

Meanwhile Jesus, our example, says to the disciples and to us, "Don't be afraid. Perfect love casts out fear." He walked freely, lived freely, and carried on an intimate relationship with the One who sent him into the world. Throughout the nights or early in the mornings Jesus spent time communing with the One who loved him. Among his last words he tells us, "As the Father has loved me, so I also love you. . . . If you keep my word, the Father and I will come to you and we will make our home in you. . . . I will send you my Spirit, who will dwell with you forever, and will remind you of all I have said to you." Jesus came to convince us that

Some old men came to see Abba Poemen, and said to him:

"Tell us, when we see brothers dozing during the sacred office, should we pinch them so they will stay awake?"

The old man said to them:

"Actually, if I saw a brother sleeping, I would put his head on my knees and let him rest."

From *Desert Wisdom* by Yushi Nomura, ed., 1982, Doubleday, New York, p. 17.

Our Maker's love is pure gift, unearned and free.

We are free to relate with the Source of all life or not.

A greater love embraces all the love that you and I have ever known, from father, mother, spouses, brothers, sisters, children, teachers, friends, partners, or counsellors.

Welcoming unconditional love automatically makes us more like the Unconditional Lover. Divine love lasts forever.

The prodigal son story is an amazing image of how God patiently waits to be in communion with us. Even if we leave home for a while, Love waits for our return. We may condemn ourselves, but we are not objectively being judged for our misguided decisions, nor is the One who loves us saying, "Away from me, I do not love you anymore. You are a bad person. You're going to hell." No! That response is against the very nature of the eternal Lover that Jesus invites us to know. The God of Jesus is, in the words of Thomas Merton, "mercy, within mercy, within mercy." As we receive mercy we become merciful, we become like the Father figure.

Even in all its beauty this story cannot fully articulate the great truth about how the One who created us loves you and me with passionate joy. Certain images of God from Scripture say more about the limitations of human expression and a given worldview than about the heart of the One who fashioned the universe. Since the writing of these texts our knowledge of the vastness of our universe and of our interconnectedness has evolved, so we no longer need to rely on older concepts about a God who does not offer second chances and whose compassion does not include those children who sometimes make poor choices. We do need to try to imagine the universal heart of the God that Jesus reveals to us. This is a Creator who says, "For I have come to call not the righteous but sinners" (Matthew 9:13). And through the parable of the prodigal son, the Lord of the Universe is saying to each one of us, "Don't make up speeches to give but trust my compassionate heart. Servants, bring out the best robe and put it on my child. Put a ring on her finger and sandals on his feet. Kill the fatted calf and prepare a feast. For this beloved of mine was lost and is found, was dead and has come back to life."

Yes, I left for the foreign country because I needed to get out and discover life for myself, but I ended up with the swine. I suffered and I also discovered a lot. And yes, I worked in my father's vineyards with angry feelings, but that is not because God wanted it that way. The One whose love is unconditional is saying, "I love you so much that I freely give you liberty to live and choose. But remember, all that is mine is yours. You've been always with me. My love for you is real and unchanged despite your unwise choices, so return to it and be shaped by it into my image."

Let us try to grow in our knowledge of the true Source of our lives. Let us allow this Spirit of all Truth into our hearts to dispel our fear, resentment, and hatred, and to shape our lives in the image of the Divine Lover. And let us not be scandalized because we have to return again and again. Leonard Bernstein wrote *The Mass*, an incredible opera about a priest saying Mass in a very contemporary setting. What you see is how the priest allows himself to be dressed by the people and

You prepare a table before me
in the presence of all my fears;
you bless me with oil
my cup overflows.
Surely goodness and mercy
will follow me
all the days of my life;
and I shall dwell in the heart
of the Beloved
forever.

From *Psalms for Praying* by Nan C. Merrill, 1996, The Continuum International Publishing Group, New York, Psalm 23, p. 40.

then lifted up, central, important, and like a very highly respected and adorned royal person. Suddenly he falls and as he tumbles downward the chalice and the plate are broken and shattered. Next you see that same priest, now dressed in blue jeans and walking amidst all the shards of broken glass. He makes an incredible statement. He says very slowly, "I never knew how bright the light was until I saw it here in the broken glass." It wasn't being lifted up that enlightened him. It was in the broken glass and in the shattered image of himself that he recognized the light of his true identity.

So homecoming for us is turning away from pervasive fears that cripple relationships, imprison us in misery, and steal our freedom. Our return means that we also recognize the light of truth in the broken shards of our individual lives. We are but fearful children, unable to relate faithfully, intimately, and permanently with Divine Love. But, constantly forgiven, we have power to love others more.

Jesus' whole mission in coming to live among us was to call us home to the truth of our lives. He lives and teaches belonging in the womb of Unchanging Love, in the intimacy of Companioning Presence, in the house of the giver of Life and Breath, in the name of the Compassionate Creator. God's name is our home, our dwelling place. When asked, "Where are you?" you answer, "I'm home. I'm in the name and that is where I live and find safety." From this home with the Guiding Spirit we walk out into the world without ever leaving this source of belonging. The name, the home, the family, the womb, and the communion are where we dwell, rooted and held.

How do we welcome home our lost brothers and sisters? By running out to them, embracing them, kissing them. By clothing them with the best clothes we have and making them our honoured guests. By offering them the best food and inviting friends and family for a party. And, most important of all, by not asking for excuses or explanations, only showing our immense joy that they are with us again. . . . The past is wiped out. What counts is the here and now, where all that fills our hearts is gratitude for the homecoming of our brothers and sisters.

From *Bread for the Journey: A Daybook of Wisdom and Faith* by Henri J. M. Nouwen, 1997, Doubleday, New York, entry for July 3.

"You do not belong to the world," Jesus said to the disciples. "I do not belong to the world. I belong to the Father." Jesus is saying that he is totally and completely living in an intimate relationship with the Divine and that there is nothing in him that isn't held in this embrace. He knows that he is sent into the world to offer us the same gift. We, too, live in the intimate embrace of the Holy One. Like Jesus, we do not belong to the world but to the Divine Comforter. And we are sent into the world just as Jesus was sent into the world to freely offer our love to others and to personify that love is possible.

Jesus draws us all into the heart of Love. "I go to my God and to your God." When we are in the heart of the Divine we are also in the heart of the world, because the world dwells in the heart of its Creator. It is from the heart of Love that we finally step into the shoes of the God figure and become compassionate lovers of others in the human family. From our dwelling place in the heart of Love we are free, we can be generous and welcoming while always remaining at home.

Listening

Listen to Love speaking to you through the ages.

"Do not be afraid for I have redeemed you. I have called you by your name. You are mine . . . since you are precious in my eyes and honoured and I love you. Do not be afraid, for I am with you." (Isaiah 43:1)

"I call you friends because I have made known to you everything I have learned from the Father." (John 15:15)

Holy Spirit, Lord of life,
From your clear, celestial height,
Thy pure beaming radiance give.

Come Father of the poor,
Come with treasures which endure,
Come Thou Light of all that live.

Thou of all Consolers best,
Visiting the troubled breast,
Dost refreshing gifts bestow.

"Anyone who loves me will keep my word, and my Father will love him, and we shall come to him and make a home in him." (John 14:23)

"It is to the glory of my Father that you should bear much fruit and be my disciples. I have loved you just as the Father has loved me." (John 15:9)

"Love your enemies, do

good to those who hate you, bless those who curse you, pray for those who treat you badly." (Luke 6:27–28)

Listen with all your heart.

Journaling

Write your willingness to forgo living from your wounded past, and step courageously into the shoes of the One whose heart is filled with love for each person. Write of your desire and willingness to gently open yourself to compassion for those whom you fear. Write of the people in your life and of ways that you will try to embrace them more as brothers and sisters on the journey of life with you. Write of your readiness to allow your maternal and paternal gifts to flower in the service of others.

Thou in toil art Comfort sweet,
Pleasant coolness in the heat,
Solace in the midst of woe.

Light immortal Light divine,
Visit Thou these hearts of thine,
And our inmost being fill.

If you take your grace away,
Nothing pure in us will stay,
All our good is turned to ill.

Heal our wounds our strength renew,
On our dryness pour thy dew,
Wash the stains of guilt away.

Bend the stubborn heart and will,
Melt the frozen, warm the chill,
Guide the steps that go astray.

Thou on those who evermore,
Thee confess and Thee adore,
In thy sevenfold gifts descend.

Give us comfort when we die,
Give us life with Thee on high,
Give us joys that never end.
Amen

Paraphrased by Henri Nouwen in original manuscript tapes; attributed to Pope Innocent III, published in 1570 in *Catholic Encyclopedia*.

Communing

Speak now to the God who has spoken into your life. Ask the Great Awakener to open the sealed reservoir of compassion, forgiveness, and welcome to all those in your life today. Speak and listen for gentle reassurance. "Fear not. Abide. Come home. Dwell in your deepest soul."

Heart speaks to heart.

Practice #9   ASK FOR SUPPORT

Far from home and isolated, the young prodigal was hungry and thirsty for food, but also for a helping hand to reclaim some of what he had lost by leaving home. He was able to overcome his load of guilt and shame, and to turn back toward home and family where he would ask for the necessary support to stand again and repossess himself in truth. His elder brother had not yet come to terms with his need to accept support in the places of his vulnerability. Both, however, were invited to grow into the parental role.

Because of being unconvinced that I am loved, I cling to my strong negative emotions as safety measures. My pattern is to fall back from good resolutions, make a faltering return, and then quickly leave again. After my breakdown and during my time in Winnipeg I knew that, despite my sense of shame, I needed support. Two people accompanied me through those long and lonely months, listening and offering consolation and questions. I cannot imagine where I would be had they not been there. Today other friends know me when I am well and when I am not so well and I meet regularly to share about my leavings, my returnings, and my increasing desire to be home to welcome others like myself.

The spiritual life is a treacherous undertaking that we best not attempt alone. In some traditions this discipline is called spiritual direction. Good mentors are themselves on this road, so they are not shocked to hear us say how often we return and then leave again. Directors listen, help us clarify motivations, and recognize destructive patterns. We want to find mentors who don't judge us or tell us what to do. We need people who encourage us to reach within for our own directions for the future, and who challenge us to stand up and reclaim love as our heritage. Good mentors point us toward truth as well as toward our many brothers and sisters in the human family who are waiting to be welcomed home by our compassionate love.

Epilogue

home tonight

Thank you, Henri, for telling us what God spoke deeply into the painful and impenetrable places in your life. Thank you for revealing the door to *our* most intimate story, and for giving us the freedom to walk our

We do not have to be saviours of the world! We are simply human beings, enfolded in weakness and in hope, called together to change our world one heart at a time.

From *Becoming Human* by Jean Vanier, 1998, House of Anansi Press, Toronto, p. 163.

own walk into the parable. Thank you for teaching us to "stand in" our pain and with integrity live it in solidarity with others in the world who suffer, and for pointing us to the small ways of claiming home while "on the way home." Thanks, too, for the gift of the spiritual practices and workouts that move us slowly into the same intimate relationship that Jesus enjoyed with the One who sent him into the world.

Did you ever realize that by so honestly sharing your identification with the two young people in the parable you unwittingly *became* for us the loving father figure, passionately awaiting *our* return to the truth?

Maybe you only ever superficially heard John's question, "Henri, are you home tonight?" But perhaps his persistent repetition supported you to courageously stumble through your second loneliness so you could return home to Daybreak. There is nothing superficial about the way you confidently invite us to do likewise. Thank you.

And now, we editors grant you, Henri, the final summary of your response to John's question, "Are you home tonight?" It is an edited quote of you speaking in the PBS documentary *Journey of the Heart: The Life of Henri Nouwen*:

> "When I saw the poster of the Rembrandt painting with the returning son being embraced by his father, I was totally overwhelmed and I said, 'That's where I want to be.' I began to think of myself as the runaway son wanting to return home. But then . . . the older son suddenly started to speak to me. I'm the oldest son myself and I recognized a lot of resentment in me, a lot of not fully enjoying where I was in my life. I woke up to the truth that both *those young people* lived in me.
>
> "More than a year later something incredibly important happened for me. I suffered from depression and was on a long sick leave from L'Arche Daybreak. One member of my community came to visit me and in the course of the conversation she said, 'Henri, you're always talking about yourself being the prodigal son, and you're often talking about your-

self being the elder son, but now it's time for you to become the father! That's who you're called to be.'

　"Look at the father figure in the painting. This person has the hand of a mother and the hand of a father, the male hand and the female hand touching a beloved child. Look at the figure of a father who is like a mother bird with a big cloak to safely enwrap her young close to her body. Look at the one who wants to welcome the child home without asking any questions. The father doesn't even want to hear the story of the younger son. The father doesn't even want to hear the story of his elder child. He simply wants them 'home,' around the same table with him, growing up to become like him.

　"In a moment I suddenly realized that my final vocation is not only to return home but also to welcome people home by saying, 'I'm so glad you are here! I'm so glad you're here! Come now. Bring out the beautiful cloak, bring the precious ring, find the best sandals. Let's celebrate because you've finally come home!' "

I stand with awe at the place where Rembrandt brought me. He led me from the kneeling dishevelled young son to the standing, bent-over old father, from the place of being blessed to the place of blessing. As I look at my own aging hands, I know that they have been given to me to stretch out toward all who suffer, to rest upon the shoulders of all who come, and to offer the blessing that emerges from the immensity of God's love.

From *The Return of the Prodigal Son* by Henri J. M. Nouwen, 1992, Doubleday, New York, p. 129.

The original talks by Henri Nouwen are
available for listening on the HenriNouwen.org website,
or for purchase through Daybreak Publications at
pubs@larchedaybreak.com.

Permissions Acknowledgments